APPROACHES TO SEMIOTICS

edited by

THOMAS A. SEBEOK

assisted by

DONNA JEAN UMIKER

21

SEMIOTICS
AND HUMAN SIGN
LANGUAGES

by

WILLIAM C. STOKOE, Jr.

1972
MOUTON
THE HAGUE · PARIS

LIBRARY OF CONGRESS CATALOG CARD NUMBER: 71-173380

Printed in Belgium by NICI, Printers, Ghent.

PREFACE

Human sign languages have been studied philosophically in the eighteenth century, pedagogically in the nineteeth century, and once or twice linguistically in the twentieth. There is yet justification for a semiotic view of the subject. Sometimes miscalled 'the sign language', sign languages are systems of signs that human agents produce in the visible mode. The signs signify different kinds of things, and the relations between sign and signified are also subject to wide variation. Semiotics, the study of sign systems, has a breadth of view somewhat wider than that of linguistics, the study of human communicative systems with vocal symbols.

A strictly semiotic exploration of the whole subject would include studies of nonverbal behavior, of a multiplicity of codes and consciously employed signalling systems, and perhaps of the complete score of the unspoken parts in the symphony of human communication. Interesting as this exploration might be, however, it is wide of the purpose of the present volume. The term 'sign' in sign language might justify such a broad excursion, but the term 'language' is a reminder that sign languages constitute a special class of semiotic systems. Because there are sign languages that possess the traits of languages proper, and because language is a very special class of anthroposemiotic systems, the central purpose will be to examine those sign languages which come closest to performing for human beings the functions performed by any natural language.

The population using one or another of these sign languages is not inconsiderable; most estimates place the number of those who cannot hear and so cannot use directly monitored speech at about one in one thousand. Even if these estimates should be overlarge by a factor of two, the number who use a sign language would still be astonishingly large. The number of persons who know what a sign language is like, how it relates to other languages and to other semiotic systems, is much smaller; for those who know it best are its 'native speakers' and lack direct experience of hearing another speaking just as most hearing persons lack direct experience of using visual symbol systems as native language. While the examination of sign languages in this volume, particularly that in use in the United States, will be directed to increasing hearing persons' knowledge of sign language, it is hoped that deaf users of sign language will ultimately benefit as a better understanding of their language is made available. To them then the work is dedicated with appreciation that without them it could not have been done.

I owe particular thanks to students in my courses in applied English linguistics and sign language grammar: Eugene Bergman, Virginia Covington, Paul Crutchfield, Hilda Richey, Betty Mahan, Marvin Sallop, Sue Wolf, Judy Williams, and James Woodward. Like all efforts in linguistic and semiotic science the present one is a collaboration, and I single out these among many informants and collaborators because our regular dialogues over two years added a special continuity. Acknowledgement is made also to colleagues in the Washington Linguistics Club and the Center for Applied Linguistics. Another source of data on the differences of sign sentences and English sentences that say the same thing is the work of the Gallaudet College Drama Department, and I am especially grateful to George Detmold and Gilbert Eastman for their careful recording of on the spot occurrences.

Finally I wish to thank Thomas A. Sebeok for his understanding editorship, for the knowledge of semiotics I have gained from him, and for his patience with my mistakes. A special thanks too to Jean Lawler for invaluable help in preparation of the manuscript.

May 1970   WILLIAM C. STOKOE, JR.

CONTENTS

CONTENTS

1

A SEMIOTIC VIEW OF SIGN LANGUAGES

A semiotic system consists of sensible things called sign vehicles, of intelligible things signified by them called sign denotata, and of the relation between the two. Language is a special kind of semiotic system. It has a small closed set of sign vehicles, but these do not directly signify anything like what is called meaning. Instead combinations of them form another set of signs, large, non-denumerable, open, full of meaning — the sentences of a language. Any two human beings in the world (with statistically small exception that will interest us later) will be found to use, as vehicles of their communication, such features as vocal cord vibration, oral and nasal resonance, air friction, tenseness in the throat and their opposites. But only if both of the two happen to speak the same language will their use of the few elemental features of all language sounds enable them to exchange messages. On the other hand, if two human beings who speak mutually unintelligible languages have time, patience, and the inclination to do so, they may learn to translate from one language to the other, i.e. learn to speak each others language. This is apparently not the case with semiotic systems generally. Different species of fireflies are receptive only to the flash pattern of another of that species even though that of a different species is different only by milliseconds (Sebeok, 1970). Social factors are involved too. Though of the same species *(Apis mellifera)*, the German honey bee and the Italian honey bee are unable to understand each other's honey locating dance (Sebeok, 1963). Yet chemical and visual semiotic systems do transcend specific and generic divisions. Many animals are able to identify prey or predators by scented 'messages'; and the work of Darwin, Chase, Ekman, Friesen, and Marler shows that the human species retains to some extent the kind of semiotic systems found in other species; e.g. visual displays of aggression, submissiveness, challenge, and the like may be understood by wolves, chimpanzees, dogs, men, and other species. Man alone has language; but man also has with the rest of the animal kingdom tactile, visual, and chemical systems of the simpler sort.

This two part proposition, that only man has language but has also more animal-like communication systems has not always been clearly understood. And the greatest misunderstandings seem to arise when the object of attention has been a human sign system called sign language. Of course, the term sign is here used with two meanings, first in the general semiotic sense already defined and second in the sense of a visible action, or gesture. A sign in this sense is a gesture, but not all gestures are this kind of sign, and it will be shown in the course of this discussion that a number of things not usually counted as gestures are part of the sign vehicle of signs in sign language.

Two major misunderstandings of the semiotic nature of sign language appear contradictory of each other as well as inconsistent in themselves, as is often the case with popular fallacies. The first is that human gestural signs are universally understood. It includes a concession that two persons can communicate in language if and only if both know the same language, but it also includes a supposition that if the two have no common language they can yet communicate 'through signs'. The fallacy lies in assuming simplistically that human gestures always denote the same thing and the same kind of thing to any signer and sign addressee because they are members of the same species. This amounts to a belief that there is a simple, constant, and species specific relation between the gestural vehicles and what they denote — That a dog's tail wag is understood by all dogs. Such relations between sign and message are what semiotics explores, and exploration shows that they are anything but simple.

When two persons not having a common language do resort to gestural communication they are not using a sign language. They are making *ad hoc* use of certain characteristics of semiotic systems. Some gestures used as signs in these circumstances function as icons, having a similarity of some kind to their denotata that is soon grasped by trial and error if it is not immediately transparent. Some gestures — many in the circumstance being considered — are indexes. They point to or are in some way contiguous with the signified. And some gestures are rapidly learned to be signals, i.e. signs that control or trigger behavior in the receiver. The most useful signals in the kind of gestural exchange in question are those which may be interpreted as, 'no; don't go on like that; you misunderstand'; and 'yes; you're getting the message; keep on'. Once the receiver of these understands them thus and the sender understands that he does, the *ad hoc* semiotic system is well under way. Like players in that form of charades known as the Game, these gesturing partners become more and more skillful fairly rapidly in the use of icons, indexes, and signals. With frequent practice they may become adept and memory may persist of the relation of vehicle to denotatum. Garrick Mallery (1881) is correct in observing that persons who use gestural communication regularly as do Plains Indians, deaf persons, and Neapolitans find less difficulty in this kind of exchange than is experienced by persons who do not. However, he is quite wrong in concluding that this observation constitutes proof of a single, universal, human sign language.

Since Mallery, a great many observations of persons in cross-cultural contact indicate something which should be implicit in semiotics and linguistics: that the difference in degree that such practice makes in no wise amounts to the difference in kind between an *ad hoc* use of gesture and a linguistic use of gestural signs. Occasions like international games for deaf athletes produce just as many halting, non-linguistic exchanges between participants as do the better known Boy Scout Jamborees and Olympic Games. At the 1968 meeting of the World Federation of the Deaf six different interpreters worked at the same time to put the proceedings into as many different sign systems for different national delegations.

The second misunderstanding of the proposition, that only man has language but man has semiotic systems of the simpler sort, over-stresses the separation. It supposes that because some human responses to gestures, to emblems, displays, signals, icons, indexes, extra-linguistic vocal noises, to scents are quite like the responses of lower animals that therefore these signs that man uses too are related to the responses in a fixed, because biologically determined, way. Those who make this mistake therefore attribute, whether explicitly or not, gestures as sign vehicles to a subhuman, zoosemiotic system. They argue from the supposition to the conclusion that systems using such vehicles cannot be language-like or human. They reverse the argument also and argue that since the systems are not language to use them is to be less than human. What they overlook besides elementary logic are the facts that man uses one mode of sign vehicle, voice (which he shares with primates, mammals, vertebrates), in language and that man having done the former has the potential to use other sign vehicles that are not exclusively his in an exclusively human relationship with their denotata.

One such use of a vehicle shared with animals in a human way is Kinesics as defined by Birdwhistell (1952). This is a language-related system of bodily actions including gestures and static positions as well to signify messages auxiliary to the language exchanges they accompany or momentarily substitute for. They may reinforce, qualify, or even deny the explicit message in the linguistic channel. Another such system is Paralanguage as Trager (1963) defines it. It has much the same relation with language messages as does kinesics but uses sounds and manners of making them as vehicle. Proxemics as defined by Hall (1959) seems to be closer in pattern to zoosemiotics and less directly related to language messages, though it is without the slightest doubt a highly developed human system.

It makes little difference, however, whether those who misunderstand sign language know these three human systems that have vehicles shared by animals. If they do not, they remain firmly convinced that gestural communication is infrahuman. If they do, they argue that the key to all three is language as speech, a view that linguists generally concur in, but they insist too on the corollary that only those with functional hearing and speech know language, a view that this semiotic study of a sign language will attempt to dispel.

The correction of this misunderstanding calls for the full examination of a sign system that does qualify as a language. Briefly stated the correct view comes from recognizing that a small closed set of distinctive features of bodily action, having no meaning in themselves, combine to form an open, larger set, the sentences of sign language. This examination will occupy the first part of this book.

Another way to know what a sign language is like is to review a number of other anthroposemiotic systems which use similar vehicles, looking at signifier, relation, and signified. At the nearest point to system-congruence with other species' behavior patterns are the expressions people's faces assume and bodily attitudes taken when they are physically attacked or threatened or put under stress in other ways. These signs may be taken as symptoms, i.e. signs denoting the state of their producer (human, anthropoid, or vulpine; see Marler, 1959), or as symbols, i.e. signs denoting fear, anger, or the like to an observer of their producer. These and many more are meticulously described and classified by Ekman (1969), who quite correctly calls all of this 'non-verbal behavior'. It is human, much of it pancultural, and it also reaches well down in phylogeny. It is social behavior undoubtedly, but it is common to all social animals. It constitutes the basic, biological stratum of anthroposemiotic behavior, and if not associated with human behavior of other kinds, if not dependent on language for its integrating infrastructure — consider the accounts of children reared by wild creatures — it would need to be classified as zoosemiotic.

Next, but a quantum jump away, are all the culturally determined systems of behavior that must be learned. These systems utilize expressions, gestures, and other bodily maneuvers (made of the same distinctive features as those just considered) to signal, symbolize, indicate, resemble, display, and symptomize denotata that are more specialized than the emotions or affects of the basic system. These denotata have to do with age, status, attention, sexual invitation and response. So listed the denotata may seem to be those of the basic system which signifies among other things the pecking order of a bird flock or the domination hierarchy of a wolf pack (Marler, 1959). But as kinesics, a culture specific behavior, these denotata are of a different order of subtlety and complexity, if as has been said they belong like their vehicles and their relation in a communicative complex with language as its central strand. This then constitutes an anthroposemiotic stratum, in one sense distinct from the basic stratum, yet using for its sign vehicles precisely the same material.

The same material is used a third way, not by all members of the human species, but by no one not a member of that species. There is now a single exception to that statement. Washoe, a four-year-old chimpanzee, appears to be using gestures in this third way (Gardner and Gardner, 1970), and the whole question of symbolic behavior is as a consequence under revision.

The third way of using the same material which serves for the expression of emotion, and for the non-verbal and paralinguistic ancillary to language, is of course to use it as the distinctive features that make the signs which constitute the sentences of a language, a sign language.

The signs of a sign language are gestures as that term is commonly understood, or misunderstood. What differentiates signs from gestures that are not signs is syntax. They occur in phrases and sentences. Similar or identical gestural phenomena which are not signs signify messages which need no parsing because the vehicles have no syntactic structure; each one means what it means by virtue of being what it is. Signs, however, in a sign language, mean what they mean by virtue of relation to other signs used with them as much as by being signs.

What makes all this difficult to describe clearly is the mixing of levels or strata that commonly occurs when persons communicate visually. Gestures used kinesically and gestures used in a more basic non-verbal manner are not any way labelled as such to mark them off from the linguistic or verbal signs. No more in speech are interjections, also incompatible with syntax, nor paralinguistic grunts, hems, or uh-uh-uhs. The native speaker of a language of course knows out-of-awareness how to respond to each sign system appropriately. But the non-signing observer is given few cues for sorting out the systems necessarily preliminary to examining the syntax of the sign sentence. Observation of actual sign language activity is made more difficult by many signers' practice of interspersing fingerspelled words with signs (one specialized gesture for each letter), of switching from sign language syntax to English syntax, and from doing both. Additional difficulty comes from the possibility that the sign language activity being observed may be on different style levels (Joos, 1961). All this of course is difficulty in the nature of the data and quite apart from the misunderstandings, sometimes willful, which have been discussed above.

The first division that the discipline of semiotics makes in its field separates language and language-based communication from non-human communication, anthroposemiotics from zoosemiotics. The sorting principle used is valid — only the human species has the semiotic system language; but the division is not mutually exclusive. Members of the animal kingdom communicate chemically by scent and taste but cannot use language. However man in all his cultures has not only had language but also used natural and consciously contrived scents for various messages. With visual signalling systems too there is one-way overlapping of the dividing line. Many of the higher animals from the birds to the great apes have a social system based on what in human settings are voice and gesture. For many species a more or less elaborated set of calls, cries, chirps, barks, howls, and so on serves many vital functions in the life of individual and species. One such function is calling; and when the call is uttered and has its effect, two or more individuals are placed where visual observation of each others actions, or where tactile communication, supersedes vocal interaction. Man's language performs all these functions and many more, but this is not to say that man has ceased to communicate by gesture and touch.

Nevertheless the indisputable validity of the first division does tend to obscure the nature of a true sign language. Language is the central fact found on the human side and not on the other side of this division.

Hence other semiotic systems, shared with animals (chemical, tactile, visual, and the rest) become in anthroposemiotics ancillary to language. There is no such thing as a simple signal on the anthroposemiotic side. To one of Pavlov's dogs a bell was, after conditioning, the cause of a flow of saliva. But to language users a bell may signal such messages as 'There's someone at the door', or 'I wonder who's phoning at this hour?' or earlier in our history, 'Who has died? For whom is that bell tolling?' A human use of gesture, kinesics, often reinforces what a speaker is saying to add meaning to his utterance; it can also deny or discredit the message in the words; but it is never independent of language if only because its use can be asked about and explained in language. Like paralanguage, the 'tone of voice' and other phenomena of performance, it has been made part of the whole communicative complex which language with its vastly more elaborated system dominates and informs.

Even more obviously, writing systems are subsidiary to languages and directly derived from them. Methods of indirectly representing the elements of the writing system, certain codes, are at still another remove from the primary system. Besides Morse and other telegraphic codes, the manual alphabets used by deaf persons are such tertiary symbol sets. In these a configuration or placement of one or both hands represents a letter, which in turn represents a segment of language sound. The existence of such codes for fingerspelling and the fact that they are commonly used by deaf persons in conjunction with true sign languages have led some observers to confuse the two. Semiotically considered the difference between fingerspelling and a sign language could hardly be greater. Fingerspelling presupposes a standard language, then an alphabetic system of writing it and a convention for spelling its words uniformly, plus a convention for giving each alphabetical symbol a manual representation. Sign language is a language with visible symbols. Its visible symbols are organized and fitted into a morphological system that combines them into meaningful units and the morphemes into syntactic constructions. In addition both morphemes and constructions are uniquely related to a semantic system that encompasses everything the users of the language communicate and think about.

The difficulty such a language poses to the traditional semiotic classification is complex. First, the nature of the primary symbols of a true sign language: they are phenomena that appear in two places in the classification. On the zoosemiotic side, actions of the limbs and body are direct signals — for instance, a certain combination of display and movement means, 'Get out of here; this is my place.' But it means this only in certain circumstances and from and to only certain participants in this zoosemiotic relationship. It is semiotic, communicative behavior, but it is not language. On the anthroposemiotic side, the material which is used for sign language symbols occurs usually also not as language but as language related, language amplifying, kinesic activity. Second, if the classification is rigidly adhered to, one or another absurdity is the result: either human sign language is treated as a special form of non-human visual semiotic, or it is treated (though it is not) as subordinate to and directly derived from the unique prime of anthroposemiotics, vocal language. Third, intellectual absurdity in the former instance leads to inhumanity. Each age has its own fashions in inhumanity. In the era of religious controversy deaf mutes were treated worse than animals because they had no speech and so were supposed to have no souls. In the modern world deaf children are judged by their proficiency in writing, reading, speaking, and understanding the language of their judges; and to explain the disappointing result, deficit theories of learning are postulated. Unfortunately, in the other instance, the treatment of deaf persons' sign language as a surrogate for speech, the absurdity also leads to prejudicial treatment. Either the sign language is said to be a very imperfect and defective copy of some other language, or the persons who use it are found by well-meaning psychometrists to have inferior mental abilities, defects in reasoning power, or communicative deficits.

Escape from these dilemmas comes from a slightly different look at semiotics. The first division remains unchanged; anthroposemiotics and zoosemiotics are still the two main branches; but the former should be at once divided into a major and a minor branch. Again no change will appear in the major branch, but in the minor branch language will now be sign language. The symbols of this language are not the calls and cries of the animal kingdom linguistically organized, as in the major branch, but the actions and displays of the animal kingdom just as linguistically organized.

As one follows down the major branch of the new classification certain semiotic activities are found. Drama, for instance, is language-related. The dance is not. The minor branch is similar to but not an exact duplicate of the major. Sign language drama is also language-related but so may be dance. Many of the movements of interpretive dancing done by deaf performers are, or are made to resemble, morphemes of sign language. Music for the hearing majority is anthroposemiotic but not related to or dependent on language directly. There appears to be no counterpart to music in the minor branch, but this is to be accounted cultural deprivation, not neurological or linguistic deficit.

It hardly needs repeating that the great majority of mankind have language as primary semiotic system, or that language uses as its basic symbols sounds produced by the same physiological mechanism possessed by many other creatures (though the high degree of human modification of vocal sounds is beyond the capability of the most intelligent of the other primates — Kellogg, 1968). What the proposed new classification adds to the picture is the important fact that a minority of mankind, those with severe hearing impairment, especially those born deaf or deafened in infancy, may have as primary semiotic system a language which uses as its prime symbols visible actions of the same kind used by many other creatures for signalling and used by the majority of mankind as supplementary or subsidiary semiotic devices.

The definition given by this proposed reclassification leaves some of what are usually called sign languages still labeled as speech surrogates in the major branch. Persons under a vow of silence in a religious community, Indians of certain American tribes, widows of Australian aborigines in their first year of mourning, and others who have been reported as using a sign language are all semiotically in the majority. Sign language for all of them is an acquired activity, and, most important, it has been acquired long after the habit of using a more usual language is ingrained. The gestural communication they use is not in the slightest degree likely to replace spoken language as their primary system of communication and thought. The same can be said of most hearing persons who associate with the deaf and use their sign language, with the possible exception of the hearing children of deaf parents. The difference is essentially that between native language competence and knowledge of a second language acquired later and under special conditions (Cicourel and Boese, 1970).

Garrick Mallery (1881), writing on Indian signing and MacDonald Critchley (1939), writing on gesture, made broad surveys of the human use of overt somatic activity for communication. The scope and focus of this work will be different. It will examine in considerable detail the thesis that there is an anthroposemiotic system which can be called language with no distortion of the term and concept but which has visible instead of vocal symbols. It will attempt to show that one sign language at least, the language of signs of the American deaf community, or American Sign Language (ASL), is a true sign language. It will use other sign languages only for illuminating comparison or contrast with this one. It will review the primary symbols of this language (Stokoe, 1960), their combination into the morphemes of the language (Stokoe, Casterline, Croneberg, 1965), the constructions using them or syntax, and so far as is possible the semantic system, both as it connects to the foregoing and as it encompasses the world as sign language users see it.

The preceding paragraph might have been written in an alternate terminology: It will be the purpose here to examine the syntactic structures of ASL, the morphemes or lexical items that may be substituted for the terminal symbols in these structures, the transformations that supply surface structure from deep structures, and the machinery needed to present all this in visible form. Or the paragraph might have taken some other language theory as starting point: semantic generation, stratification, tagmemics, etc. The approach chosen does make a difference in what one finds to say about the substance and the relations of a language, and consideration will be given to a number of competing theories of language and their suitability for sign language analysis.

Since a language community using sign language exclusively and not in contact with other languages does not exist, bilingualism and diglossia (Ferguson, 1959) will need careful consideration. Most users of sign language operate with a two-channel communication system of great variety and complexity. When one channel receives visible language symbols and the other visible facial manifestations of, or surrogates for, vocal symbols, the whole system may operate with a simultaneity not common in bilingual situations; and attention to the whole semiotic complex as it actually operates may shed some light on problems of multiple language occurrence.

Such considerations lead to a more general view of the whole matter, and this study of sign language will conclude with a brief discussion of the questions of epistemology raised by a language with visual symbols instead of the usual case when asking how we know what we know.

REFERENCES, CHAPTER 1

Birdwhistell, Ray L.,
   1952 *Introduction to Kinesics* (Washington, D.C., Foreign Service Institute).
Chase, Richard Allen,
   1966 *Evolutionary Aspects of Language Development and Function* (Baltimore, Johns Hopkins University Neurocommunications Laboratory).

Cicourel, Aaron V., and R. Boese,
    Forthcoming "Sign Language Acquisition and the Teaching of Deaf
    Children", *The Functions of Language,* ed. by Hymes *et al.* (New York,
    Teachers College Press).
Critchley, MacDonald,
    1939   *The Language of Gesture* (London, Edwin Arnold).
Darwin, Charles,
    1873   *The Expression of the Emotions in Man and Animals* (New York, Appleton).
Ekman, Paul, and Wallace V. Friesen,
    1969   "The Repertoire of Nonverbal Behavior: Categories, Origins, Usage, and
    Coding", *Semiotica* 1:1, 49-98.
Ferguson, Charles A.,
    1959   "Diglossia", *Word* 15, 325-340.
Gardner, Beatrice T., and R. Allen Gardner,
    1970   "Two-Way Communication with an Infant Chimpanzee", *Behavior of Non-
    human Primates*, ed. by Schrier and Stollnitz (New York, Academic Press).
Hall, Edward T.,
    1959   *The Silent Language* (New York, Doubleday).
Joos, Martin,
    1961   *The Five Clocks* (New York, Harbrace).
Kellogg, W. N.,
    1968   "Communication and Language in a Home-Raised Chimpanzee", *Science*
    162, 423-427.
Mallery, Garrick,
    1881   "Sign Language among North American Indians", *First Annual Report of
    the Bureau of American Ethnology*, ed. by J. W. Powell, 263-552.
Marler, P.,
    1959   "Developments in the Study of Animal Communication", *Darwin's Biolo-
    gical Works,* ed. by P. R. Bell (Cambridge, Cambridge University Press), ch. 4.
Sebeok, Thomas A.,
    1963   "Zoosemiotics", *Lg.* 39, 448-466.
    1969   "Semiotics and Ethology", *Linguistic Reporter,* suppl. 22, 9-15 (partially
    reprinted from *Approaches to Animal Communication,* ed. by Sebeok and
    Ramsay [The Hague, Mouton, 1970]).
Stokoe, William C., Jr.,
    1960   "Sign Language Structure: An Outline of the Visual Communication Systems
    of the American Deaf", *SIL:* O.P. 8 (Reissued Washington, D.C., Gallaudet
    College Press).
Stokoe, William C., Jr., C. Croneberg and D. Casterline,
    1965   *A Dictionary of American Sign Language* (Washington, D.C., Gallaudet
    College Press).
Trager, George L.,
    1958   "Paralanguage, a First Approximation", *SIL* 13, 1-12.
West, LaMont, Jr.,
    1960   "The Sign Language: An Analysis", Unpublished Ph. D. Dissertation
    (Indiana University).

2

WORDS, SIGNS, AND SYLLABLES

The natural point of entry for the observer of another language than his own is the word. The word is in the middle of the morphological system of a language which itself is midway between the phonological and the semological systems (Trager, 1963). That entity of a sign language which corresponds with word is the sign. Every observer of sign languages since antiquity has discussed sign language as signs, whether describing the circumstances of their use, explaining their appearance, or glossing their meaning. But of course the observer of sign language who is also a linguist is aware that languages have the unique characteristic Hockett (1958) calls 'duality of patterning'.

It has been apparent since 1960 that the signs of American Sign Language (ASL) are morphemes, i.e. that the elements that compose them are relatively meaningless bundles of distinctive visible features distributed in the language in ways closely analogous to that system designated by the term PHONOLOGY. The name given to these distinctive feature bundles or isolates or structure points of the language is CHEREMES, /kériymz/; and they have been found to form three classes called TAB, DEZ, and SIG (Stokoe, 1960). The ways in which they differ from phonemes in operation are as important as the similarities.

Leaving aside for the moment lexical or semantic considerations, an ASL sign may be regarded as the counterpart of a syllable in speech. Both are minimal performable units. Vowels and consonants have pronounceable names, but these are syllables in which conventional additions are made to the isolated sound to make it syllabic. Sign elements too are smaller than the smallest sign. They do not divide segmentally into vowels and consonants but aspectually into place markers, tabs, configurational markers, dez, and action markers, sigs, all of which may be visible at the same time. Yet like segmental phonemes, these constituents of signs cannot be performed in isolation. A tab cannot be indicated without using a hand which itself becomes a dez even as its action of indicating becomes a sig. Even when a distinctive hand configuration, a dez, is shown or presented, the act of presenting it constitutes a sig, and the place where it is presented becomes its tab. Thus just as a letter name pronounced is a syllable, a sign aspect signed by a signer is a sign (though it may not be a lexical item of this language).

At this point the comparisons between sign and word and between sign and syllable must be dropped and attention given to another relation between sign language and languages of the more familiar kind. Those who use American Sign Language also have a quite different system which employs distinctive hand configurations. This system, called fingerspelling, differs radically, i.e. semiotically, from sign language, for hand configurations in it represent alphabetical symbols. The whole set of them is called a manual alphabet. There are two principal kinds of these: using one hand or two; and there are varieties of each, historically and geographically distributed; but one particular one-hand manual alphabet is known and used by those who also use American Sign Language. Since a great deal of effort at precise description can be saved by showing them, the hand configurations of the American manual alphabet are illustrated in Fig. 1. It is well to keep in mind that the difference between fingerspelling with a manual alphabet and using American Sign Language is not exactly the same as speaking a language and writing a language with alphabetic symbols. The latter two activities are related in ways that are becoming better known (Reed, 1966; Lotz, 1969). The former two are only superficially related. A signer using American Sign Language is producing its cheremes, its morphemes, its sememes, i.e. its sentences and its longer units of discourse. However when he fingerspells, a person is encoding written English by a one-for-one system of hand shapes for letters, following conventional orthography exactly, and for as long as the fingerspelling continues switching off the production of sign language.

It is well to keep all this clearly in mind because in spite of this linguistic and semiotic difference of sign language production from the fingerspelling of English, all discussion and teaching American Sign Language and all written accounts of it use frequent reference to the manual alphabet — more particularly to the relation of hand as sign to letter as signified. The reasons for this practice, which has greatly confused the whole semiotic nature of 'deaf sign talk', are not hard to find. The hand configurations of the manual alphabet are readily illustrated

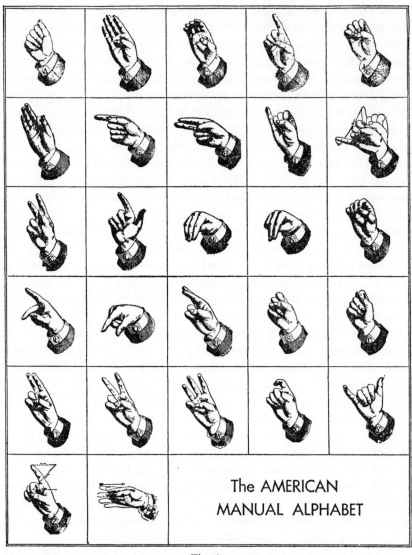

Fig. 1.

(almost every American English dictionary has a cut of them). The code is easily learned. It is most convenient then to refer to the hand configuration by the letter conventionally associated with it. Moreover the convention is stable (Abernathy, 1959).

The whole history and description of manual codes for alphabetical symbols is a subject for a separate study but only connected to the study of a true sign language through the material of the signs, not through the system relating them to their designata nor to the designata themselves. Nevertheless there are two reasons for considering somewhat further the fingerspelling of those persons who also use American Sign Language. First, semiotically considered any manual alphabet can be a sign language, though its designata are strikingly unlike those of natural languages. It will be apparent from Fig. 1 that the hands for *d* and *z* are identical. Viewed as sign language, fingerspelling the letter *z* uses the *d*-hand as dez. Tab is the place where the hand is held for fingerspelling. And the sig of the sign for *z* is a movement which traces a *z* with the fingertip. But viewed thus, *d* is also a sign; its sig is simply presenting the *d* dez. The same relation holds for the two letters 'signed' by the *i*-hand. Presented only the *i*-dez is *i*; tracing a *j* as sig makes it 'sign' the other letter. Still looking at Fig. 1 and fingerspelling as a kind of sign language, *h, n,* and *u* all have the same dez, the two fingers extended touching. Presenting them pointing upward, downward, and to the side are the sigs for *u, n,* and *h* respectively. The hands for *a, s,* and *t* differ, but subtly. If distance, light, or movement make it difficult to distinguish them, all three will be a single dez — and movement, of course, is a feature of the sigs of American Sign Language.

The second reason for inclusion of this simple hand-to-letter code in a discussion of American Sign Language is linguistic. It serves both as a bridge, a middle language, between English and sign language and as a system by means of which words of English are borrowed and at the same time transformed into true signs either as permanent additions to the ASL lexicon or as nonce coinages. Personal and place names too in American Sign Language use the manual alphabet-fingerspelling convention as the first step in a completely sign language process. It was stated above that the cheremes of American Sign Language are 'relatively meaningless'; so most of them are; but when an *r* hand is brought to the mouth in the same way a different dez is to sign 'eat', the R-dez sign also carries a reminder that it came into the language from the ten letter word *restaurant*.

One convention which will be regularly followed here is already introduced and should help to keep reference to the two systems, signing and fingerspelling, distinct. Lower case letters will be used for the hand configurations of the manual alphabet, but upper case letters in roman type will refer to hands which function in American Sign Language as dez or tab.

With this caution it is possible to return to the comparison of a

sign to a syllable, especially a syllable of CVC type. The two consonants
and the vowel of such a syllable are linguistic elements which have
received enormous amounts of attention from antiquity to the present,
and there are certainly competing theories to account for their nature
and function, but one thing about them is hardly controversial: the fact
that they can be symbolized CVC represents agreement that they are
segments of speech ordered in time as the contrast of *tip* with *pit* in
English and our left-to-right spelling convention make redundantly clear.
A sign has already been written of as a combination of tab, dez, and sig,
and may be (and hereafter will be) symbolized TDS; but this reduction
of sign cheremes to letters is misleading. Equally adequate cover symbols
for a sign would be DTS, SDT, TSD, DST, and STD. Order, in other
words, is not a feature of sign composition. Cheremes are not segments
but aspects of a sign. Segmentation of a syllable or other act of speech
is temporal division. The analysis of an ASL sign must be aspectual,
i.e. spatial, because cheremes are different aspects of the same sign act.
A TAB by definition is a distinctive marker of sign place, but it is also
the place where a dez does something. A DEZ is an active element
distinguished from other such by visible features, but it is seen in,
at, on, against, or otherwise related to a tab. A SIG is action or motion
which differs from other such action, but a sig is only a sig by being
the action of a dez 'in' a tab. A sign differs from a syllable, then, in that
all of its constituents may be simultaneously present to the attention
while the segments of a syllable are in sequence.

Another difference is that only accidental constraints restrict the
occurrence of consonants in initial and final position in a CVC syllable,
e.g. English has /biŋ/ but not */ŋib/. Signs however are not signs unless
all three aspects are present, i.e. there are two sets of segmental phonemes,
consonants and vowels, but three sets of cheremes, tabs, dez, and sigs
(for both euphony and typographical elegance the plural of *dez* is not
given herein as *dezzes*).

Although the aspectual cheremes are distinguishable, there is a way
in which as sets of cheremes they overlap. The same hand configuration
which is dez when it acts, i.e. performs a sig, is tab when it is held and
is acted upon by the signer's other hand; e.g. the I-hand (see *i* in Fig. 1)
made by most right-handed signers with the left hand is tab, and the
I-hand, right, is dez in the sign glossed 'last' or 'finally'. The sig is a
downward movement of the dez so that the right little finger strikes
the left in passing. Because it is possible with comparison of minimal
pairs to establish that downward motion (v) and the act of touching

or striking (x) are both sigs, this sign has two simultaneous sigs and is written : I I $^{\vee}_{x}$. Other signs in which both hands have the same configurations or different configurations occur in two ways. One hand may be tab and the other act as dez, as in 'last', or both hands may act in performing the sig, in which case the tab is NEUTRAL-TAB or ZERO-TAB, symbolized ϕ, the space in which the dez operates when no other tab is overtly marked. Thus there are not only signs described by the cover symbol TD^S and TD^S_S but also T DD^S. Indeed, since sig actions may be performed in sequence or simultaneously, sig cover symbols alone are: $\frac{s}{}, \frac{s}{s}, \frac{ss}{}, \frac{ss}{s}, \frac{ss}{s}$, and $\frac{ss}{ss}$.

While the foregoing is at least a schematic presentation of sign language morphocheremics before a full discussion of the cheremic system of the language, the spatial aspect of signs and the temporal segmentation of syllables constitute so important a contrast that it seems advisable to thus anticipate the description of sign language cheremes.

Two other points must be considered in the contrast of a sign and a syllable. A syllable consists of more than vocalic and consonantal segments. As a pronounceable unit of language, whether it be a morpheme of a language or nonsense, a syllable when produced has with it, over it, around it, or in it non-segmental or supersegmental features as well. Whether these are considered as automatically generated by phonological rules of the speaker's grammar or as phonemes of stress, pitch, and juncture which like segmental phonemes are used in the language to make elemental contrasts and so to affect morphology and meaning, they are observata, data to be handled. A sign too is more than its tab, dez, and sig cheremes, and this is a fact which has not received nearly enough attention from anyone who has heretofore written about American Sign Language. General advice has been given to those who would learn the language, often in a negative precept: "Don't sign with a wooden face." On the positive side, it was noted (Stokoe, 1960) that the action of a signer's head, face, and eyes can be taken as signals of a question, a statement, and a negation. But the implication of both seems to be that facial expression or motion of the head function in sign language in a way analogous to an intonation contour. The semiotic and anthropological insights of Sebeok and Sarles (in Stokoe, 1970) point to a need to consider American Sign Language less narrowly as what the hands do and in fact as all that is visually observable in a communication.

Examined thus, American Sign Language has more signs than have hitherto been recorded and more ways of making them than are outlined in the discussion of cheremes above. It is possible to view the formation of words in English as analogous to sign language morphemics, whether one takes *contract, v.,* and *contract, n.,* to be the result of a phonological rule working by a transformational cycle on a syntactical structure (Chomsky and Halle, 1968) or as the morphemes: $k.\acute{a}.n.\vdash$ and $°t.r.\acute{æ}.k.t.,$ combined with either of these morphemes: lexical microfix ($^{\upsilon \cdot}/\cdot$) or lexical macrofix ($/\cdot /\cdot$) (Smith, 1968). Either way, and the choice still seems to be aesthetically determined, segmental and supersegmental elements constitute distinct phonological, lexical, and grammatical linguistic signs. But this analogy will only account for such pairs as 'remember' (indicative, with nod or downcast eyes) and 'remember?' (interrogative, with questioning look) or 'enjoy' and 'didn't enjoy' — the same manual sign with headshake (Stokoe, 1960: 61-62). A better analogy might be Chinese in which tone as well as segmental phonemes must be specified. But even here the analogy is faulty because sound and sight are not analogous. If a stress combination or a tone could be uttered without the production of any vocalic or consonantal sound either would bear a closer similarity to what a signer's face may do. It can actually divide the labor with the hands, expressing not only linguistic signals like 'question', 'negative', 'command' and stylistic modifications signifying all kinds of things that kinesics and para-language do (Trager, 1958), but also lexical items like *I, you, he, she.* Of course one does not need to be a user of American Sign Language to know that messages like 'Yes', 'No', 'I don't know', 'Don't bother me' can be sent and received with no vocal signs at all, but it should not be surprising to learn that deaf persons who may carry on all the activities of a very complete culture use all kinds of visible activity as elements of their dual-patterned communicative system.

Because it is a recent discovery the detailed discussion of the facial component of American Sign Language will be presented in a later chapter. What follows is a description of the manual, cheremic, system.

2.1 CHEREMES

Although any one of six orders might be chosen for the representation in arbitrary symbols of American Sign Language cheremes, the one adopted in *Sign Language Structure* (1960) and followed in the *Dictionary* (1965) is tab, dez, sig, or TDs. This chapter is therefore arranged in the same order.

The tab first in frequency is the zero or neutral tab, ϕ, which contrasts with all specifically marked tabs and is best described as the place in front of the signer's body where the hand or hands can be moved easily and naturally. Next, to make an arbitrary decision to read from the top, there is the upper part of the head, tab $\cap$. When signs are described in words instead of being shown in photographs and drawings, the writer usually gives very specific directions, e.g. in 'hat' the fingers touch the top of the head; in 'know' the fingertips meet the middle of the forehead at an acute or right angle; in 'black' the index is drawn across the brows. Such precision in the location of the sign activity is analogous to a very narrow phonetic transcription. But the object here is to describe the cheremes, an operation analogous to phonemic description. All three of the places touched in the signs described above are allochers of the same tab.

Below this tab is mid-face, $\wedge$, with eyes, nose, and the space in front of them as allochers. Whether in signing the dez actually makes contact with that part of the body serving as tab is to some extent a stylistic matter. As in proper paralinguistics (Trager, 1963) variation both sides of a mean can be significant. Deliberate and precise contact of dez with tab allochers marks a stilted performance. Loose approximation of the tab regions is characteristic of informal and intimate styles.

At about the same height but with allochers covering a larger area is the cheek or side of face tab, 3. And with this tab the difference between actual contact and sig motion in the vicinity is allocheric in part. The sign 'girl' — drawing down (sig) the ball of the thumb (dez) along the cheek (tab) — usually involves a light grazing touch; but the sign 'refuse', which could be described as a sharp jerk of the thumb over the shoulder, usually does not. Contact in the former sign is hard to avoid owing to the musculature and acticulation of the arm. It is easily and wisely avoided in the latter as a scratched cheek could result.

The lips, mouth, and chin are in the area of tab $\cup$, lower face. Written descriptions of signs again are more specific: the mouth for 'eat', 'say', 'thanks', but the lips for 'red' and the chin for 'beard' and 'shave'. As all six signs may be made with the dez hand an inch or more away from the face, it is clear that meaning rather than accurate observation is the governing consideration in the usual descriptions of ASL signs.

The whole face is also a tab. Signs like 'dark', 'beautiful', 'shock' bring the dez hand or hands in front of the face, $\bigcirc$, rather then one of the just cheremically specified parts of it.

The throat region and the side of the neck are both touched or approached in several signs, but only one tab chereme need be recognized, neck, Π. When 'voice' is the sign, the fingertips of the V dez straddle the throat. When 'broke' is signed the edge of the dez B (flat hand) makes a chopping motion toward or against the side of the neck. In each case the sig and dez together select the suitable allocher of tab Π, very much as a front and back vowel in English select a light and dark allophone of /l/.

The whole trunk region is a single tab chereme, symbolized [ ]. Though the actual allochers chosen may be as far apart as the shoulder and the hips, no signs are made to contrast by simple difference in placement on the trunk. There is always a dez difference or a sig difference or both, so that again the choices of allochers of chest tab is governed by complementary distribution. This is not to say that all variation observed in the actual region touched, approached, or indicated is complementery allocheric distribution. Women generally use higher allochers of this tab and men lower, but the style level too has an effect. Really colloquial, particularly male, sign talk is low down: the abdomen may be touched in signing 'have' while a formal female signer may touch the collarbone. Indeed the English stylistic term *gut-level* applies aptly to the informal signing style of males in the same social group.

The upper arm is distinguished from the lower and acts as a single tab, ᴠ. The allochers of this tab chereme vary from the center of the biceps muscle in 'coke', 'shot in the arm', to the whole length of the biceps in 'strong' and to the side of the triceps in 'Scot', 'Scotland', 'Scottish'.

The angle of the elbow and the outer side of the upraised forearm form another tab, $\sqrt{}$ with these two allochers also in complementary distribution. But the lower half of the forearm, the wrist and hand, presents a more complex cheremic arrangement.

When the hand is turned in supination (palm upward) the proximal side of the wrist is in position to be tab. Allocheric variation allows any part of the surface presented to be used. In pronation the tab area is larger since the back of the hand makes an extension of the wrist surface. Allochers of tab are correspondingly spread over a larger space.

But this does not come near to a full catalogue of tab cheremes. The hand, with its multiple articulations within itself and freedom to be tipped and rotated, not to mention its evolutionary history of semiotic employment — the hand is also quite productive of ASL tab cheremes. Note that its power of making kinds of movements in many manners is not being overlooked here but will be treated under the aspect of signation. More properly it is both dez and sig, both the hand's movement and its articulateness, that are important in the physical manifestation of sign language. Indeed the separation of the three aspects, tab, dez, and sig, is an act of analysis. All three are integral parts of signs; and as the discussion of complementary distribution has indicated, dez and sig together can affect the choice of a particular allocher of the tab. The analysis being attempted here is actually a conscious try at separating aspects which occur together; and while it may be a useful linguistic practice, it is probably no more certainly to be established by strict empirical methods than is the segmentation of the flow of speech.

All this is a complicated preamble to a description of the hand as tab in American Sign Language, but the matter itself is complex. A hand used as tab is after all a dez hand held still while the other hand, truly dez now, performs a significant action. And when the hand is under observation in the activity of signing, other matters interfere. The hand in various configurations is also the active element in fingerspelling, and while the latter is a symbolization of the alphabetical symbols which represent language sounds, and while signing uses direct, though non-vocal, language symbols, the fact is that practically the two are mingled. Not only do deaf persons in the ASL community mix finger-spelled words with sign morphemes, but they also coin signs; and the language has received such coinages since 1776 (Stokoe, 1960: 11f.) by a method which blends fingerspelling with signing. Initial dez signs (Stokoe, 1965: xxv) are made by taking the manual configuration for the initial letter of the word to be translated and using it as dez; it is then given a tab and sig and so is made a true sign, but an intermediate stage may be recognized. Manual spelling is kept as free of abbreviations as is formal written English, but certain frequently occuring words, especially proper nouns, may be abbreviated by holding the initial letter configuration or slightly shaking or circling or pushing it forward. In this case the tab is neutral space and the sig is the slight movement. Such signs might be considered fingerspelling abbreviations as contrasted with true initial-dez signs like 'wine' — the w-hand makes a small vertical circle with index fingertip against cheek; or 'Danish', the d-hand makes a small circle with the nails touching the forehead.

As to the hands or configurations themselves, the following occur in either tab or dez aspect:

The hand made into a ball or fist contrasts in ASL use with other tab-dez hands but not with itself. Receivers of fingerspelling must distinguish three similar hand configurations: a, the thumb against the side of the curled fingers; s, the thumb crossed over the front of the second phalanges; and *t*, the thumb inserted between first and middle fingers. But all three of these and more (the thumb upraised from the fist is given a diacritical mark, $\dot{\text{A}}$, though the difference is non-cheremic) are allochers of a single chereme, A, used as tab or dez. The convention adopted when the symbols for ASL cheremes were devised in the late fifties was to use the letter for the configuration of the manual alphabet nearest an important allocher of the ASL chereme — with upper case to distinguish the chereme from the letter in fingerspelling. Thus in transcribing actual communicative activity the ASL morphemes are easily distinguished from fingerspelled words which are represented in lower case italics. In describing signs with written symbols, a letter (from the manual alphabet) is a convenient way to indicate a particular allocher. Thus A_t represents an ASL chereme physically identical to a manual *t*, $A_s = s$, $G_d = d$, and so on.

To remain within the alphabetical convention, the next chereme is given the symbol B from the *b*-hand of the manual alphabet. However the chereme B has several allochers and the B_b allocher (thumb across the palm) is statistically least important. Perhaps it would be more accurate to say that the position of the thumb is exactly specified by the conventions of fingerspelling but that the distinctive feature of the B chereme is the plane of palm and fingers. Flat or slightly curved, continuous or broken by slight separation of the fingers, the plane is what makes a hand the B chereme — the position of the thumb is unimportant. But quite apart from configurational differences which are allocheric here, the B chereme is presented as dez or tab in many positions. Whether any pair of these makes a cheremic contrast is not easily answered. Remember that tab, dez, and sig aspects are all combined, not strung out in sequence, to make a sign morpheme. The convention adopted when the dictionary was compiled (1965) is to use subscript symbols to distinguish minimally contrasting pairs.

Thus 'school' and 'money' written without subscripts seem homophenous: $BB^{x\cdot}$ (the tab B, dez B touches tab, and this sig is repeated). With subscripts 'school' is $B_aB_p{}^{x\cdot}$ (tab B held palm up, dez B, palm down, touches tab twice); and 'money' is $B_aB_a{}^{x\cdot}$ (... dez B, palm up, touches tab twice). This convention of writing the cheremes attributes the contrast entirely to the different orientation of the dez in the two signs, but it would be just as true to say that the sig of one is a forehand strike and the sig of the other is a backhand. Since the existence of the manual alphabet makes hand cheremes easier to symbolize than motion cheremes the former course was adopted.

A very noticeable difference, even seen at odd angles and from a distance, between the flat hand and the same hand with the fingers spread as far as possible makes a cheremic distinction. The spread hand is not used in fingerspelling but is the manual symbolization of the numeral five, and is therefore given the arabic numeral, as symbol, chereme 5. Another difference between B and 5 as ASL cheremes is that when dez contact with tab is involved in the sig, the dez chereme 5 almost always makes the contact with the thumb tip and the dez chereme B almost never, but uses palm, back, edge, or fingertips.

The third letter of the alphabet also associates with a hand configuration used as a chereme in ASL morphemes. The C chereme as tab or dez opposes the curved fingers to the curved thumb. Seen edgewise this configuration resembles the letter 'C' (or its mirror image), but seen as a chereme of American Sign Language it provides an open or nearly closed ring as well — a tab into which or out of which the other hand as dez may move significantly.

The manual alphabet d is used as subscript to the chereme symbol G, index finger. As may be supposed the index hand is much used in signing, but as manual alphabet g is more nearly like the index hand in configuration, 'G' is used as the chereme symbol, and d as subscript when the index extends above the circle made by the thumb opposed to the three remaining fingers. This subscript is also used when G dez makes contact not in the usual way with index tip or edge but with the joined nails of thumb and curved fingers.

The fifth letter, $e,$ is represented in the manual alphabet by a configuration used for a few signs as dez. As these are initial dez signs and as the chereme is not used as tab, it may be supposed that E chereme is an ASL addition not likely to be found in nineteenth century American Sign Language nor in the French Sign Language, its immediate source.

The hand configuration which extends and spreads the three outer fingers while thumb and index finger meet forming a circle is the chereme symbolized F. Some Americans use this for f in fingerspelling. Others stay closer to the pictured manual alphabet (Fig. 1) by bending the index finger at right angles to the palm and crossing the thumb over it at the second joint. The French and Irish deaf, who use a similar alphabet, make f with crossed thumb and index and use the three finger and circle hand for g. This chereme too is much more frequent as dez than as tab and in fact the tab occurrences of which the *Dictionary* (1965: 252) lists four are variants of double-dez signs, that is signs with neutral tab and both hands acting as dez.

The next chereme, both tab and dez, has already been introduced after C, but it is important enough for double mention. Just as pointing or indicating is an important part of anthroposemiotics both as kinesic, out-of-awareness language-related signalling and as overt communication, so pointing as sig and the index or pointer finger as dez are important in American Sign Language. Many of the pronouns of other languages are translated in American Sign Language with G dez signs. Such is the construction of hand and arm that the index can be pointed in any direction in three dimensional space. Held upright it needs no larger sign to indicate unity, 'one'. Moved upright from another position it has the force of 'once'. And of course it is used for fundamental directions up, down, to, there, here, and for many other signs.

The configuration made by the index and middle fingers extended, sides touching, is given the symbol H as an ASL chereme, though it could have been given *n* or *u* as well as *h*. In fingerspelling the position of the hand is all important for some letters, *h* being made with the fingers horizontal or obliquely held and *u* pointing upward, while *n* requires the fingers to bend down over the thumb. But in ASL use the function of the dez is not just to contrast with other dez cheremes but to move, to perform a sig, so that depending on the tab and the sig used with chereme H, the fingers may move through all the manual alphabet positions for *h, u,* and *n* and others as well.

The *i* hand of the manual alphabet as chereme I is used as tab in a few signs — the *Dictionary* (1965: 262f) lists six — and as dez in several others. Some of the latter are initial dez signs while others appear variants of signs using G chereme in some dialects or idiolects. It seems likely that this chereme like E (and K which follows) is a late addition to the ASL cheremic system. Thus a simpler description might be made by counting G and L as allochers of a single chereme and doing likewise with E and A or E and X and with K and V. But it should be remembered that productivity is an important feature of language (Hoijer, 1969). Coinage of initial dez signs makes it easy for ASL users to keep up with accelerating cultural change. And while ASL cheremics probably will never evolve to the stage where the sign addressee will have to make the minute visual discriminations demanded by fingerspelling, it is also realistic to assume that every manual alphabet configuration (there are twenty, not twenty-six, because of positions and movement in fingerspelling) potentially may become dez of a newly coined sign.

All these considerations apply to chereme K, otherwise the *k* hand of the manual alphabet. Held pointing up as *k,* it is initial dez for signs

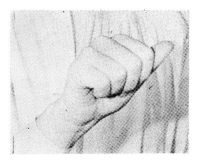
Tab Ø   Dez A

Tab Ⓤ   Dez √B⊤

Tab ⌒   Dez 5

Tab ⊔   Dez C

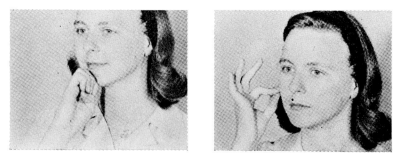
Tab ∪   Dez E   Tab }   Dez F

Fig. 2.1.

Tab ⊓   Dez G   Tab [ ]   Dez L

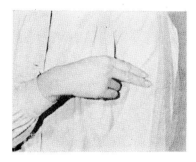 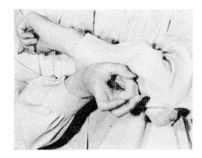

Tab \   Dez H   Tab ✓   Dez V̈

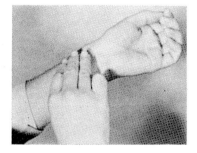 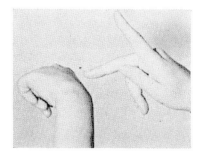

Tab ⊔   Dez W_D   Tab Ɔ   Dez K_v

Fig. 2.2.

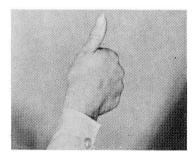

Tab Ø   Dez Ȧ

Tab Ø   Dez √B

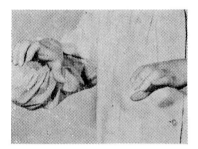

Tab Ø   Dez C𝒟 C𝒟

Tab Ø   Dez G> G<

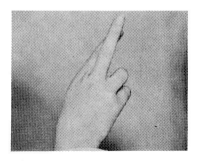

Tab Ø   Dez R

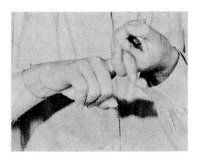

Tab Ø   Dez X^Ⅱ X

Fig. 2.3.

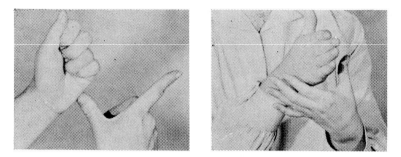

Tab <u>A</u>　　Dez L　　　　　　　Tab B$_a$　　Dez B

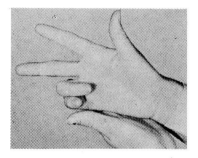

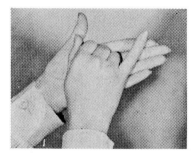

Tab B̄$_a$　　Dez 3˙　　　　　　Tab B̄$_a$　　Dez Y$_D$

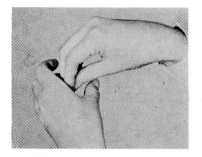

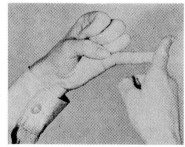

Tab C　　Dez O$_v$　　　　　　Tab I　　Dez G

Fig. 2.4.

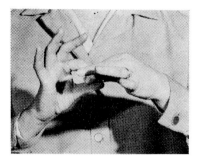

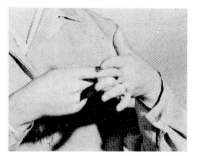

Tab Ø   Dez F^{II}F

Tab 5°   Dez G

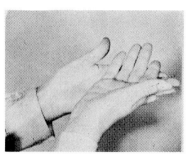

Tab B$_a$ Dez B$_D$

Tab B$_a$ Dez B$_a$

Tab ∪   Dez Ȧ

Tab B$_a$ Dez Ċ$_D$

Fig. 2.5.

Tab $\overline{A}$ Dez A

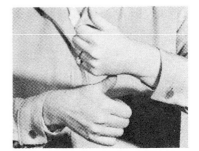

Tab $\underline{A}$ Dez $\dot{A}$

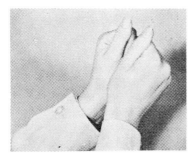

Tab Ø   Dez A^{I}A

Tab Ø   Dez A$_\circ$ A

Tab Ø   Dez B† B

Tab Ø   Dez √A†√A

Fig. 2.6.

 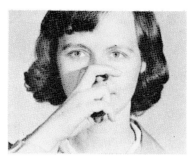

Tab Ø   Dez √G_a   Tab ⊔   Dez V̈̈

 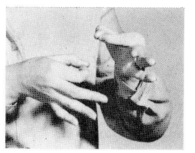

Tab · B¹   Dez B̈̈   Tab Ø   Dez F F

Tab ∩   Dez B<   Tab ∩   Dez A<

Fig. 2.7.

like 'king' and 'keep', downward it is initial dez for signs that translate words beginning with *p*: 'principal', 'principle', 'Philadelphia'. As tab the K chereme occurs as a variant of the pronated forearm chereme D or of the X hand. The *Dictionary* lists only two signs with K as tab (1965: 264). In both these the tab hand appears to have been attracted into the K as initial dez in 'keep' and 'perfect'. Thus eliminating K from the set of cheremes would be a possibility since these two signs may be called allocheric variants of signs with D, X, and V cheremes. In fact the configurations *k* and *v* can be distinguished only when seen from certain favorable viewing angles. Even in fingerspelling they need not be visibly different because of the distribution of the two letters in English words. And in ASL use as in any language a lack of physical intelligibility of a submorphemic symbol is immediately compensated by the redundant features of the language or supplied by the addressee from the semantic pattern. But in spite of all these points in favor of describing ASL cheremics with fewer cheremes the argument that has prevailed is that of productivity.

The L chereme too has initial dez sign uses, but as tab its essential feature is the angle made by thumb and forefinger. This feature appears whether the other fingers are folded in, as in American manual alphabet *l* (some European alphabets use the following form), or held extended in a plane.

The remaining cheremes used either as tab or as dez are O, V, W, and X. Those used as dez only are 3, R, Y, and 8. The hand for spelling *o* is usually held so that the fingers and opposed thumb form a fair approximation of a circle. As an ASL chereme, however, the O hand has much more freedom, varying allocherically from the circular to an elongated, tapered shape or to a configuration identical with the manual alphabet *m* or a bent *b*. As tab, especially with sigs that involve moving the dez into or out of the encircling O chereme, it is indistinguishable from some allochers of the C chereme.

The *v* hand of the manual alphabet is also the V chereme of American Sign Language, but fingerspelling requires its upright presentation while cheremic use allows or requires it to assume any position.

The *w* hand and the W chereme differ from the *v*/V hand only by the extension of a third finger, but this difference is distinctly visible and is useful for many initial dez signs. (Only one sign with W tab is listed in the Dictionary and that may often appear as zero tab sign with both hands in W as dez.)

The *x* hand of fingerspelling displays the index finger bent into a hook.

The X chereme has this formation as one of its allochers and as the other the same with the thumb tip pressed against the index fingertip.

Two of the cheremes used as dez only are R and Y. Initial dez signs using R chereme are fairly numerous. The hand in *r* configuration held up and moved slightly to the side makes a sign found both in American Sign Language and in general American kinesics with the same significance: 'I'm keeping my fingers crossed' is the verbal equivalent, that is, 'May what (I, you, he) said (etc.) turn out all right.' No exact survey has been made, but the writer has the distinct impression that this sign is more frequent of occurrence among sign language users than in speech communication in comparable situations. It would seem likely that a context of signs makes a more suitable condition for its survival and use than a context of spoken syllables. Nods and headshakes are not exactly comparable, since they have a simpler significance.

The alphabetic configuration *y,* which makes an opposite extension of thumb and little finger from the otherwise folded hand, is one allocher of Y chereme used as dez in many signs. Some of these are initial signs like 'yellow' and 'New York'. Others are representational and still more simply arbitrary uses of the Y dez — more of this in the discussion of morphocheric structure below. Another allocher of Y keeps the ends of the configuration outstretched while the three intervening fingers wiggle (though sometimes only the middle finger is seen to move).

Of similar appearance is an allocher of the chereme symbolized 8. Physically there may be no difference but subjectively one 'feels' Y as two points and a mass in the middle, 8 as a plane-like hand with the middle finger pointed at right angles to the plane. The other important allocher — in complementary distribution: it appears when sig calls for a sudden change of 8 to 5 — catches the nail of the middle finger under the pad of the thumb preliminary to the snapping open sig. Interestingly the sign 'pity' uses the pointed finger allocher on both hands (in zero tab, the sig calls for moving the fingertips in small circles) while the sign 'hate' uses the caught-nail allocher (both hands in zero tab snap the middle finger outward). Although authorities on the psychology and education of the deaf have called ASL signs "ideographic" (Myklebust, 1964: 235f) and "by and large ... suggestive of the shape, form, or thought which they represent" (Davis-Silverman, 1960: 419); neither linguistics nor semiotics affords a description of how these two emotions look in reality nor of the ASL, sign-like appearance of any idea.

This concludes the enumeration of tab and dez cheremes which are comparatively easy to describe and which can be illustrated by photographs or perhaps better because more generally by drawings. The chief difficulty in dealing with them lies in determining exactly the level of analysis. A strict cheremics of sign language would perhaps reduce the number of cheremes, but devising a set of graphic symbols not only to depict them in isolation but also to reflect to some extent ASL users' feelings about sameness and difference in signs has from the outset accompanied the analysis.

It is harder to describe sig cheremes and analysis of them is even more subject to the instrumental error caused by intruding a graphic symbolism into a purely somatic, non-vocal, though semiotic system of distinctive actions. All this is but an elaborate way of expressing dissatisfaction with the analysis represented in the 1960 and 1965 publications; not that they are not useful and discriminating enough for many purposes, but that both linguistic and semiotic science require a better and more recent description of the relations between the units of this language.

The first step in all such description is to ask 'what?' But even in stating what sign language action is, scholars of the past and today interpret 'what' in two divergent ways. Bebian's *Mimographie, ou essai d'écriture mimique propre à régulariser le langage des sourds-muets* (1825, cited in Stokoe, 1960: 15) and Schlesinger and Peled's (1967) work seek to show by systematic diagrams and graphical conventions what angles, arcs, planes, directions, heights, widths, and other dimensions the signer's hand or hands move in. Valade (1854, cited in Stokoe, 1960: 15f.) and McCall (1965) use, respectively, French words and English words to show 'what' signs are. The former interpretation concentrates on the signifiers of the system, the latter on the signifieds. A semiotic approach calls for explication of both of these and of the system relating them within the sign language they belong to.

It would seem that in sign language, as in the more general sign systems contemplated by semiotics, the starting point would be the physical manifestation, the sign which is "not of interest in itself (as a combination of certain physical properties) but as something opposed to another concept termed signified" (Revzin, 1964, trans. Bergman). As Revzin points out it may be that the real signifiers are not the words of the natural language (or the signs of American Sign Language) but instead functions, i.e. the categories or symbols found in the rules that generate the sentences of the language. Considered in one light this may be the frankest admission yet that generative grammars are more important or more real than natural languages . But Revzin in fact advocates both generative and descriptive linguistics. And whether one starts with the sign or the grammatical category, whether cheremes are the input to the morphology or the output of the final component of a generative grammar, some attention must be paid to the sign as physical phenomenon and both interpretations of what signs are fall short.

Too close concentration on the physical attributes of the sig aspect of sign language activity may blind the observer to the non-significance of much of that activity and to the meaningless precision of his observations. It also misses significant features by omitting from observation what may accompany sig action. And of course assuming the translatability of each sign by a word of the observer's language overlays all the relations between signifier and signified that are to be discovered with largely unanalyzed relations within the second language.

Just what constitutes the symbolic, significant, semiotic portion of the whole activity observable when someone is using sign language has been defined as what the dez does relative to the tab and is called the sig. It is limited by the skeletal and muscular arrangements of human and primates (Gardner and Gardner, 1970). Differences of size, age, sex, state of health and other conditions affecting signers are variables which allow movement to appear different to an observer outside the language yet to be accepted as the same by all users of the language. Even so, the differences that these conditions impose on sig appearance — e.g. abruptness/smoothness associated with males' and females' signing style, and brisk/relaxed movement which may come from vigor or fatigue — these differences are also part of what makes a sig. The how of signing is very much part of the what. There is also a mean between these extremes. A certain manner of sig action may be simply characteristic of the signer-person — though that too signifies much. It may be cheremic, that is it may distinguish what is being signified from other meanings by its presence or absence. And between physiological and cheremic force it may instead have stylistic effect.

A table of the sig symbols (Fig. 3) may look complex enough because of its unfamiliarity and its non-geometrical treatment of sig movement; but the use of these symbols to record movement as it actually occurs, not abstractly, and the additional information not covered by these symbols that is necessary are still only part of the very complex matter of signification.

One unusual feature is the grouping of sigs in vertical, sideways, horizontal, and rotary actions. Movement upward, movement downward, and oscillating movement up and down are expressed in most treatments

Sig symbols

^	upward movement	
v	downward movement	vertical action
N	up-and-down movement	
>	rightward movement	
<	leftward movement	sideways action
z	side to side movement	
T	movement toward signer	
⊥	movement away from signer	horizontal action
I	to-and-fro movement	
a	supinating rotation (palm up)	
ᴅ	pronating rotation (palm down)	rotary action
ω	twisting movement	
ᴎ	nodding or bending action	
□	opening action (final dez configuration shown in brackets)	
⧺	closing action (final dez configuration shown in brackets)	
ℛ	wiggling action of fingers	
⊙	circular action	
)(	convergent action, approach	
x	contactual action, touch	
⹇	linking action, grasp	
†	crossing action	interaction
⊙	entering action	
÷	divergent action, separate	
()	interchanging action	

Fig. 3.

of motion and even in the normal way of stating them in English as
x, y, and x + y (when *x* is defined as the opposite of *y*), or as +, —, ±.
But the physical or spatial analysis of sign movement is not semiotic
nor linguistic analysis. Take the three signs 'raise', 'heavy' and 'perhaps'.
In all three the tab is clearly zero, both hands form the dez, B chereme
in its simplest allocheric form: the hands are held out palm up, relaxed
(that is slightly curved not extended flat). To sign 'raise' both hands
move up ($^\wedge$). To sign 'heavy' both hands move down ($^\vee$). To sign
'perhaps' both hands move up and down (^{N}) not in unison but
alternately (~). Though it is quite true that up and down motion is
the reiterated addition of upward motion and downward motion, this
truth is quite irrelevant to any linguistic or semiotic investigation of

American Sign Language. 'Raise' and 'heavy' are not unrelated semantically, and both signs translating these words may have iconic relation to their meanings; but it is immediately apparent that the simple opposition of the two sig movements has no such counterpart in the conceptual scheme. Add the sign 'perhaps' and the logical treatment of summed motions is even farther removed from anything in the sign system. Moreover 'perhaps' is but one gloss for this sign; others are 'maybe' and 'who knows?'; and in many kinesic and gestural systems the last meaning is often related to simply an upward motion of hands, shoulders, brows, or all three.

Similar sets of three signs can be found showing rightward, leftward, and right and left movement ($^>$, $^<$, ^{z}); inward, outward, and in and out movement, i.e. toward ($^\top$), away from the signer ($^\perp$), and both ($^\mathrm{I}$) — and pronation (^{p}), supination (^{a}), and oscillating twisting motion ($^\omega$). In all these cases the same results are found as in the first example: motion in one direction, motion in the opposite direction, and the combination of the two show a simple logical relationship; but sig movement so related has no isomorphism with sign semantics.

This small excursion into sig cheremics should be sufficient to disprove the idea often stated as truth rather than as hypothesis that American Sign Language is ideographic or suggestive, that its symbols are tied in some non-linguistic, deterministic way to what they signify. Why must the rapid rotary oscillation of the dez mean 'play', pronation mean 'drink' and supination mean 'other' unless because sign language has cheremic patterns and semantic patterns related as such patterns are, in linguistic duality?

This is not to say that the clear relations of one-directional, opposite and summed sig motions cannot be useful. One engaged in learning ASL vocabulary and mastering its performance may find it very helpful to remember otherwise unrelated English glosses for signs by associating them with opposite and added motions. By using the same tab and moving the dez in three easily distinguished ways the learner acquires three signs in performance with a minimum of effort. This is the method of one of the most widely used manuals for learning sign language; its whole arrangement is based on the *Outline* (1960) and *ASL Dictionary* materials (Fant, 1964).

It should also be noted here that a direction of movement and its opposite in the sigs of otherwise identical signs may relate to an opposed pair of meanings, but this relation holds between ASL syntax and semology, not between a sign and its lexical meaning.

After the twelve sigs in their three-sig groups, are listed five distinctive movements and a final group of seven, characterized by interaction between dez and tab or between the two hands in signs with double dez.

Nodding or bending action (ŋ) differs from simple vertical action by its articulation: the dez pivots at the wrist or in some cases at the knuckles of the hand. Thus nodding action has a smaller radius and need not be in a vertical plane; e.g. in the sign translating 'you and I' the dez is V or K held so that nodding sig alternately points the second finger at signer and the index at addressee (*Dictionary,* 1965: 97, where the sig is shown as to and fro motion).

Opening (□) and closing (#) action of the dez constitutes a different kind of motion from the sigs so far considered, for it causes not a change in place of the dez but a change in state. A fist may open to a spread hand (A$_s$ □ [5]). Or the 5 hand may close to an O (5 # [O]). The ASL vocabulary for cardinal numbers makes extensive use of these signs, which only incidentally are related by physical opposition and muscular contraction and extension. Again the ASL symbolism is arbitrary, linguistic, and not in any elementary sense logical. There is nothing but duality of patterning to be seen in the fact that springing three fingers from a tight fist signals '13' (A$_s$ □ [3]) while closing the 3 chereme to one or another allocher of □ signals '30' (3 #) — even though the 3 dez does show an obvious relation with the natural number three.

Small actions of the fingers singly or in rapid sequence has been called wiggling action (ᴁ). Although bending and straightening a finger as strictly described motion is longitudinal wiggling, and the rapid rippling of the outstretched fingers is transverse wiggling; the nature of any such action is so easily distinguished from nodding and other action that move the elbow or shoulder joints that it constitutes but one sig chereme. But this is stated with an anatomical frame of reference. The cheremic consideration is that nowhere in American Sign Language are two signs differentiated by difference in two kinds of wiggling action alone.

Circular sig (∂) is unmistakable when seen in ASL activity. The circle described may vary in size, but this variation is allocheric. It may be in a vertical plane as in signing 'always', or in a horizontal plane as in 'here', or in a vertical plane perpendicular to the first as in 'come' and 'go'. Nevertheless circular as contrasted with rectilinear motion is distinctive and cheremic. Again the importance of semiotic procedure is apparent. A meticulous observer of human gesture will note that unless special care is taken by the maker to coordinate several muscular sets involving more than one joint, manual movement is usually in arcs with a joint

as center. The ASL fashion of moving is the opposite: special care
(though out-of-awareness) is taken to make circular sigs very closely
approximate circles, but sigs that make quite appreciable arcs are
taken as rectilinear — at least as non-circular.

The sig symbols in the last group indicate still another way that sign
activity operates. Heretofore what has been observed is what the dez
does when the center of attention is the dez — it makes no difference
whether the attention is the conscious observation of the analyst or the
learned and out-of-awareness attention of the addressee intent on
what is being signed, the signified, instead of on what the hands are doing.
In the case of the sigs that follow, the important consideration is what
the dez does in relation to the tab; or what the two hands both as dez do
with respect to each other.

Convergent action or approach (x) and actual contact, touch sig (^{x})
are necessarily related as coordinated physical movement. An operational
definition would insist that an approach phase precedes a touch, though
action may be stopped and only the approach phase appear. Cheremic
analysis finds no such relation. Signs alike except for this difference may
signify concepts as different as are signified by words differing in one
feature such as voicing, as in 'fat' and 'fad'. As a matter of fact minimal
pairs are not easily found. The signs for 'short' and 'school' use B palm
up as tab, B palm down as dez. In the former the dez approaches and
stops, in the latter the dez touches the tab twice. But in 'want' where
the double dez hands approach the trunk and in 'have' where they
touch the chest, checking the movement in the former so that touch
does not occur makes it an almost straight pulling in of the hands and
the hands exhibit an allocher of C like a bent 5. In the latter the motion
continues smoothly until the tips of the B hands strike the chest.

However the differences in a semiotic system are not all to be found
in the lexicon. The users of American Sign Language may be said to
operate within the restrictions of cheremic contrast, but they also
operate with it as a highly maneuverable semiotic vehicle. Thus a signer
instead of using approach sig for 'small' may let the hands actually
touch to convey a humorous exaggeration of smallness. Or 'have'
may be signed with a deliberate suppresion of contact to get an effect
that a speaker might use special intonation or a writer an elaborate
circumlocution to achieve — for instance 'He has a wife'. Again like
paralinguistic phenomena (Trager, 1958), this kind of sign language
signalling seems to swing to one side of a norm or to the opposite side.
A signer who wants to emphasize possession, as after the implication

of its denial, may make the touch sig vigorously, forcibly, and repeatedly.

The comparison to paralanguage is a reminder that all this is a digression from strictly cheremic consideration of interaction sigs but also requires further elucidation. Semiotically considered, kinesics and paralanguage are as much sign systems as is the activity here being subjected to microlinguistic description. It is difficult to make any model of communication that relates kinesics and paralanguage to speech and show it isomorphically repeated in the communication of those who use American Sign Language both from choice and necessity, the deaf members of the linguistic community. The model with speech included has two physical modalities of reception, sight and hearing. The target model can have only the first; though the importance of tactile and kinaesthetic modes should not be overlooked in any psychological or anthropological study of deaf society that aims at completeness — none has yet appeared.

Nevertheless it can be argued here that the three-channel model, paralanguage-speech-kinesics, may be matched by a three channel purely visual model. The deaf signer as has already been shown operates with the signs, with sign language as the speech-like master channel which has duality of patterning. He also operates with a paralanguage-like channel of which the illustrations above of ways of signing 'small' and 'have' are evidence. He moreover operates with still another channel which is like kinesics or, it may be, is kinesics. Facial expression not required as part of sign performance and other 'body language' — all kinds of postures, movements, and displays — are not only free to contribute to the semiotic ensemble but most certainly are so used. Thus the signer can simultaneously modify the ways of making signs in a paralinguistic way and transmit a comment on the whole message in a kinesic way. It is probable that the distribution of information amount, rate, and kind among the three channels is different in spoken and signed communication, but to consider both as anthroposemiotic systems it may be better to try to describe the ensemble than to dwell on the channel separation and differences. It is certainly too early to make value comparisons.

To return to the sig aspects of signs themselves, there are other interactive movements. Taking hold of a tab or part of a tab, linking action, or grasping ($\mathfrak{x}$) varies of course with the configuration of the dez and nature of the tab. Pinching or plucking is done with dez cheremes F, and X, which use thumb and index finger, with C which closes to O, and with 8, which uses thumb and middle finger. Grasping (allocher of $\mathfrak{x}$)

occurs with C dez. Linking is done with double dez X and with the little fingers of Y. And the 5 hands and W hands may be joined by interlacing the fingers.

Similar interaction which is nevertheless distinguished, cheremically different, is crossing ($\neq$). Within this chereme the allocheric difference comes from the size of the cross: fingers, hands, wrists, the whole forearms may be crossed.

In contrast, entering action ($\odot$) makes the tab container and the dez contained. The tab hand may execute a grasping action or remain passive. Either way this sig is distinct from others. Allocheric differences come from direction of dez movement and position. The tips of the fingers enter the tab first in signing 'in' and 'ride with'. The tips of the fingers are the last part of dez to pass through the C tab in 'both' and 'gone'. The dez hand in 'enter', 'into' passes through the C tab held pronated.

Separation ($\div$) sig, considered simply as action, is opposite to five interaction sigs, approach, touch, grasp, cross, and enter. A sign pair with the same tab and dez and different only by having separation sig in one and a positive interaction sig in the other may show semantic opposition or may be unrelated semantically.

The action of interchanging ('') is also distinctive, but it requires some other sig to be used with it and it constitutes a special kind of repetition of sig action. Thus in the sign for 'friend' double dez X's link ($\mathfrak{X}$) then interchange (''), i.e. the hand that was above and the hand that was below change places.

With interchange sig the inventory of cheremes is complete, though ASL cheremics is far from completely treated. Further information about tab, dez, and sig aspects of sign language emerges when the focus of attention shifts from signs or pairs of signs in isolation to their use in actual exchanges, and to the cheremes in combination. If another word may be coined, it is sign morphocherics that now needs investigation.

Between cherology and the morphology of American Sign Language there is a set of relationships — some might call it a stratum — in which the clear contrasts seen in minimal pairs merge into moving shades. The signs made by one signer look different from the signs made by another, and the difference seems to be cheremic, yet both are apparently accepting these differences as sames. One way of making this merging less rhetorical is mathematical statement.

Cheremics, in set theory, states that the cheremes of American Sign

Language constitute a set, χ, the members of which are those tab, dez, and sig aspects described in the foregoing chapter. Thus:

$$\chi = \{\phi, \cap, \cup, \triangle, \cup, \text{etc.}, A, B, 5, C, \text{etc.}, {}^{\wedge}, {}^{\vee}, {}^{\wedge}, \text{etc.}\}$$

That χ has subsets is already obvious. These are the set of tab cheremes (T), the set of dez cheremes (D), and the set of sig cheremes (S). Sigs are motions clearly distinct from dez and tab aspects which are at least in part organic. Therefore the intersection of the sig subset with the tab subset is zero, and the intersection of the sig subset with the dez subset is zero. And the union of these three subsets is just the set of all cheremes:

$$\{T\} \cap \{S\} = \phi; \{S\} \cap \{D\} = \phi; \{T\} \cup \{D\} \cup \{S\} = \chi$$

However there are two kinds of tabs, those that cannot otherwise be used as dez and those that can. Thus the intersection of the tab set with the dez set is a set containing just those cheremes which do function either as tab or as dez — :

$$\{T\} \cap \{D\} = \{A, B, 5, C, G, H, I, K, L, O, V, W, X\}$$

The principle that a chereme is a contrasting element of sign language that can tolerate allocheric differences is also expressible in set equations. If the cheremes of a sign language are given the general symbols, Γ, $\triangle$, Σ, etc., each one is a set of allochers: $\Gamma = \gamma_1, \gamma_2, \gamma_3, \ldots; \triangle = \delta_1, \delta_2, \ldots;$ $\Sigma = \sigma_1, \sigma_2, \ldots$ — then, and this is the principle of cheremic contrast, the intersection of one chereme set with another is zero. No allocher of one chereme is an allocher of another: $\{\Gamma\} \cap \{\triangle\} = \phi; \{\Gamma\} \cap \{\Sigma\}$ $= \phi; \{\triangle\} \cap \{\Sigma\} = \varnothing$; etc.

As the focus of attention moves from the points of elementary contrast to the constitution of morphemic units, these clear relationships of contrast and exclusion are no longer pertinent. The essence of the relations at the new level (or stratum) is shown by sets that do intersect Different signers observed making the sign translated 'now' use as double dez cheremes Y or O or B. The first uses a loose or relaxed allocher of Y in which the distinctive thumb-little-finger extension appears but the intervening fingers only slightly bend. The second, seen from directly opposite the signer, uses a hand that looks very much like O in an allocher that brings the thumb up (the dez hands are all fully supinated for 'now') almost parallel with the fingers but not touching them. The third signer makes so slight a bend in the hands that to one observing cheremes, they appear to be an allocher of B. Thus if the dez of 'now' is given the symbol Q, Q is a set which has as its members the three cheremes Y, O, and B. More strictly the members are those allochers of Y, O, and B seen in three signers performance of 'now': $Q = \{Y_n, O_n, B_n\}$.

To recapitulate, in cheremics, the tab, dez, or sig of any sign is considered to be a chereme, and in cheremics allochers of one chereme do not appear as allochers of another. But in morphocheric organization, when the signs of a number of signers are viewed, the tab, dez, or sig as part of a sign morpheme is a morphocher and it is actualized with one or another chereme depending on the particular signer's dialect or idiolect.

In addition to specifying what cheremes are used to actualize the morphochers found in ASL signs the function of morphocheric analysis is to discover, classify, and record the arrangements of morphochers permitted and not permitted (i.e. not occurring) in American Sign Language. Some attention has already been given to this level of semiotic structure in noting that sometimes one hand is dez sometimes both are double dez. In the chapter which follows the terms tab, dez, and sig will still be used, but they may there be taken to refer to morphochers as just described rather than to cheremes strictly considered.

REFERENCES, CHAPTER 2

Abernathy, Edward R.,
  1959 "An Historical Sketch of the Manual Alphabet", *American Annals of the Deaf* 104, 232-240.
Bébian, M.,
  1825 *Mimographie, ou essai d'écriture mimique, propre à régulariser le langage des sourds-muets* (Paris).
Chomsky, Noam, and Morris Halle,
  1968 *The Sound Pattern of English* (New York).
Davis, Hallowell, and S. R. Silverman,
  1960 *Hearing and Deafness* (New York, Holt).
Fant, Louie, J., Jr.,
  1964 *Say it with Hands* (Washington, D.C., Gallaudet College Press).
Gardner, Beatrice T., and R. Allen Gardner,
  1970 "Two-Way Communication with an Infant Chimpanzee", *Behavior of Non-human Primates*, ed. by Schrier and Stollnitz (New York, Academic Press).
Hockett, Charles F.,
  1958 *A Course in Modern Linguistics* (New York, Macmillan).
Hoijer, Harry,
  1969 "The Origin of Language", *Linguistics Today*, ed. by Hill (New York, Basic Books), 50-58.
Lotz, John,
  1969 "The Conversion of Script to Speech as Exemplified by Hungarian", *Linguistic Reporter*, suppl. 23, 17-30.

McCall, Elizabeth A.,
1965 "A Generative Grammar of Sign", Unpulished M.A. thesis (University of Iowa).
Myklebust, Helmer R.,
1964 *The Psychology of Deafness* (New York, Grune and Stratton).
Peled, Tsiyona,
1967 *A System of Notation for the Sign Language of the Deaf* (= *Working paper* 3, project no. VRA-ISR-32-67, USDHEW).
Reed, David W.,
1966 "A Theory of Language, Speech, and Writing", *Elementary English* 46, 845-851.
Revzin, I. I.,
1964 "From Structural Linguistics to Semiotics", *Voprosy Filosofii* 18:9, 43-53. (Translation by Eugene Bergman).
Schlesinger, I. M.,
1967 *Problems of Investigating the Grammar of Sign Language* (= *Working paper* 2, project no. VRA-ISR-32-67, USDHEW).
Smith, Henry Lee, Jr.,
1968 *English Morphophonics* (= *Monograph* 10) (Oswego, New York), New York State English Council).
Stokoe, William C., Jr.,
1960 "Sign Language Structure: An Outline of the Visual Communication Systems of the American Deaf", *SIL*: O.P. 8 (Reissued Washington, D.C., Gallaudet College Press).
1970 "CAL Conference on Sign Language", *The Linguistic Reporter* 12, 5-8.
Stokoe, William C., Jr., C. Croneberg and D. Casterline,
1965 *A Dictionary of American Sign Language* (Washington, D.C. Gallaudet College Press).
Trager, George L.,
1958 "Paralanguage: A First Approximation", *SIL* 13, 1-12.
1963 "Linguistics is Linguistics", *SIL*: O.P. 10.
Valade, Y.-L. Remi,
1854 *Études sur la lexicologie et la grammaire du langage naturel des signes* (Paris).

3

AMERICAN SIGN LANGUAGE MORPHOCHERICS

By far the greatest number of ASL signs have a single tab. There are signs however in which two tabs are clearly identified because the sig brings the dez into contact or close proximity with two separate tab markers. Although the sign for '(male) homosexual' is written in the *Dictionary* (171) with a single tab ($\cup 8^{\times \wedge}{}^{>}_{\times}$), it seems to be a clear example of a two-tab sign. The tip of the dez finger touches or approaches the lips, then brushes outward the eyebrow or temple.

Other signs which suggest two tabs (e.g. 'remember') are more likely to be contractions of two-sign lexemes. Indeed some sign handbooks give the gloss 'think-seal' for the older two-sign rendering of 'remember'. Contractions and compound signs will be treated under morphemics below.

In some signs the sig is seen to begin with the dez in, at, on, near, or in some other relation to the tab. In other signs the sig ends with the dez in contact with the tab or in the closest relation it assumes with the tab. In still other signs, notably in zero tab, the same relation of dez to tab is maintained throughout the duration of sig action. For the first of these cases, several symbols are useful. These morphocheric symbols of the invented ASL writing convention do not denote contrasting aspects as cheremic symbols do but help to make more explicit the relation of chereme to chereme in the sign. A line above a tab symbol indicates that the dez begins the sig from a position on or above the tab (Ā). A vertical line between tab and dez or between the two symbols for double dez shows a side by side placement initially (B/). A subscript (q) to a chereme is used to show that the hand referred to is in front of the other hand. Symbols that normally denote a sig action are used too for those signs which begin with the hands in a particular relationship, usually before sig action separates them. Crossed index fingers the

initial position for 'but' are shown thus: G ⊹ G. The C hand holding
the fingers of the H hand is shown thus: C ⊙ H — with separation sig
'resign' or 'quit' is signed, but with the hands staying joined and moved
in (horizontal) circle sig, 'ride around (with)' is the translation of the
resulting sign. The sign for 'co-operate' has the same sig but joined F
hands (FⱯF).

Much of what pertains to dez morphocheremics has been encountered
in the description of dez cheremes, but there are arguments for making
a different separation of dez cheremics and dez morphocheremics. If dez
cheremes were to be distinguished by configuration contrast only, one
would need to count more cheremes than have been described. But if
both configuration and position or orientation are taken into account,
then some of what have been classified as sig actions belong in dez
cheremics. It must be recalled that tab, dez, and sig aspects of signs are
even less easily empirically separated than the vocalic and consonatal
segments of speech flow.

The position taken in the *Outline* (1960) and the *Dictionary* (1965)
may be justly called a compromise. Thus in the convention adopted
then, B^v symbolically describes this sign: in zero tab which does not
need explicit symbolization, the flat hand as dez turns in pronation,
palm downward (depending on context and other features of signing
it may translate 'bad' or 'bet'. But written differently (B_v) the same
symbols indicate only a dez, or it may be a tab, the flat hand held, not
turned, palm down. Again B^a may be a sign, dez B turns palm up, for
'how?' or 'why?', 'how come?' But B_a is the hand held palm up. There
is no way of knowing whether it is being used as tab or as dez when
other symbols are not found with it.

This discussion of dez and tab morphocherics has dealt with symbols
used for sign notation. These symbols have nothing to do with ASL
activity itself, which had gone on for a century and a half before the
writer introduced the symbols. But dealing with cheremes and their
combination in morphemes the use of symbols is much more economical
than filmed or video-tape reproduction and less ambiguous than static
illustrations. To continue with two of the symbols used in the examples
above, the clearest case of position alone as the contrasting feature are
the two tabs made by the extremity of the arm. The symbol 'a' represents
the forearm on its back; whatever configuration the hand is in is immaterial. The symbol is of course that for sig action of supination written
larger. Likewise the symbol 'ᴠ' represents the forearm in pronation
with the hand so relaxed usually that it forms no ASL or manual alphabet

configuration, although an athletic signer or one who does heavy work may hold the hand even in these two cheremes in a fist-like way.

One might argue after the fact that the hand configuration is not regarded in the tab cheremes a and v because sig action of the dez is centered in the wrist region, not in the more distinct parts of the hand. This leads to a further way in which morphocheric features are indicated in sign notation. Particular parts or points of tab and dez cheremes are involved in sig actions. For example A dez can touch or strike A tab in several ways. When both are pronated ($A_v A_v$) the wrist or heel of the dez hand taps on the back of the tab as in the sign glossed 'work'. When the thumb of the dez presses the thumbnail of the tab ('seal' or 'stay') a dot over the basic symbols (Ȧ Ȧ) serves several purposes. It indicates a prominent feature, the thumb, of an allocher of A chereme. It indicates the place of contact on the tab; and it indicates the point of the dez used to make the contact indicated by the sig.

Another morphocheric feature is seen in all three aspects. When the dez is higher than normal, the forearm becomes part of the dez. (Normal is defined as the place where the dez easily moves, zero tab.) When this happens the tab becomes either a high allocher of zero tab — this choice of analysis was made in 1960 — or a new tab. The sig too shows difference. Movement of the dez in zero tab is usually movement of the hand; i.e. the wrist, elbow, and shoulder joints act so that the motion is apparently rectilinear. In high zero tab, when the dez includes the forearm, sig motion moves the dez in arcs with elbow as center.

All these adjustments of dez, tab, and sig seem clearly interdependent, suggesting the complementary distribution of allophones in certain phonemic or phonetic environments. Notice of the difference could perhaps be taken in describing any of the aspects or two or all three. In the writing system adopted, however, the simple prefixing of the elbow tab symbol to the dez symbol is the alternative chosen; e.g. $\sqrt{B^\perp}$ or $\phi \sqrt{B^\perp}$ 'will', 'in the future', 'later' is a sign made with the forearm upraised. The dez arm may even be moved to its full extension outward and up, but this would be seen if (1) the signing was formal and directed to a large audience, (2) the signer in an informal sign conversation became intensely animated, or (3) the meaning was intended that calls for a phrase in English — 'way in the future' or 'much later'.

This kind of relation between signifier and signified seems to call for synthesis as well as for analysis, and morphocheric treatment to some extent supplies the need. In signing generally, tab, dez, and sig are interdependent; and semantic, stylistic, and paralinguistic-kinesic systems are also in use. As part of a semiotic system the ASL activity that denotes 'future time' or 'I will' or the sense 'later' includes meanings connected with excitement, determination and all the circumstances surrounding signer and addressee or audience. Cheremic and morphocheric distinctions serve as a necessary first phase in the investigation which will need to include stylistic, kinesic, and correlational analysis as well.

One place in morphocheric relations where more refinement is needed is in describing the sig aspect of signs. In the *Outline* (1960) and *Dictionary* (1965) the term sig was used for the totality of significant action performed by the dez in relation to tab. The following passage from the *Dictionary* (viii f.) makes this use of the term clear:

1.1 Writing American Sign Language
With the understanding that all separation of real human communication into word-size units is a little artificial, we can proceed to a representation of the separate signs of the American sign language by symbols for the three elemental aspects of a sign. If we use 'T', 'D', and 's' as cover symbols for any possible tab, dez, and sig, we can write a sign thus: TD^s. This formula or convention for writing a sign indicates that at or in some place (T), visibly distinguished from all other sign language places, a hand configuration (D), distinctly different from all others used in sign language, performs an action (s), visibly unlike all other such actions.

Not all signs are made in just this way, because the sig may be a combination of movements. Some signs will be written like this: TD§. Here two sig actions are combined; that is they are done at the same time. Thus 'down' and 'touch' (^v_x) written one above the other will indicate that the dez moves down while in contact with the tab. In other words it grazes, brushes, or scrapes down across the tab. Or two straight-line sigs, 'right' and 'down' (v̄), done together combine to make a motion downward and to the signer's right.

Another kind of formula shows the sig symbols side by side: TD^{ss}. This way of writing a sign indicates that one sig action is done first and a second follows.

A third kind of formula shows two dez symbols: TDD^s. This way of writing a sign indicates that both the signer's hands serve as a double dez. A double-dez sign like this may have a single sig symbol as shown or have a compound (^s_s) or a double (^{ss}) sig. Indeed, some double-dez signs and some with single dez may have three sig symbols ($^{ss}_s$) or (^{sss}) and some even four ($^{ss}_{ss}$).

This amounts to defining an ASL sig as a single significant action and contrasting action (Chapter 1 above) at the same time defining it as a combination of such actions either successively performed or simultaneously or both. A more consistent treatment of sig action may be offered now. It takes sigs as partially analogous to consonants, which may occur singly or in clusters. When a sign uses two different sigs one after the other, it is analogous to a word or syllable with a two-consonant cluster. A fairly frequent two-sig sequential cluster is circle sig followed by touch sig. The signs for 'when?', 'year', and 'nature' are examples.

More frequent though than tab-dez-sig signs are those with an interaction sig, then a motion sig that displaces the dez, then another interaction sig, most aften the same one repeated. Examples are 'member' [ ] $\overset{'''}{B}{}^{x<x}$ (the symbol $'''$ indicates that dez fingertips make the contact), 'million' B $\overset{'''}{B}{}^{x\perp x}$, 'improve' vB^{xTx} and its antonym, $vB^{x\perp x}$, which, partial bilinguals sometimes translate with the unedited blend 'deprove'. Signs with three-sig clusters bear a kind of pattern resemblance to three-consonant clusters, but the sequence ... $VC_1 C_2 C_1$ is hardly typical of English phonotactics.

Sigs also cluster in ways that are not strange but impossible for segments of speech as these are presently described. The physiological basis of sign language makes possible the performance of two sigs in the same brief time span. And this is not exceptional but common. In ASL terms, the hand can easily open ($\square$) from the A configuration to the 5 configuration at the same time it moves away from the signer ($\overset{\square}{\perp}$). Apart from language, every primate who has ever thrown a stone has proved how easily these actions combine. Another simultaneous clustering combines touch with other action. Such co-occurring actions when not used in language are perceived and spoken of as unitary. English has *scrape, graze, brush, slide,* and other words to describe them. Nevertheless signs using touch only as sig exist along with signs using only a simple movement, so that signs which combine them must be examples of this special kind of simultaneous sig clustering.

There is no need to limit to two the number of sigs that can be combined in simultaneous performance, though three may be as many as the present technique of description can accomodate. In the sign for 'week' the dez L moves obliquely to the right ($>$), lightly grasping the tab in passing (x), at the same time closing from L to X ($\#$). At the same time it may be observed that the tab 5 used by some signers (the *Dictionary* lists B tab) also closes. But this is not necessary to symbolize; it is not cheremic; and the sign would be the same even if a signer had an immobile artificial hand to use as tab. Still all these actions may appear, and all are cheremic; they contrast when used as single sigs. Typographical limitations of course make it necessary to write one of the three combined sigs as if it was performed later (i.e. $B_a \, L_{>\,>}^{\,\mathfrak{X}\#}$: *Dictionary*, 241, 236).

Two sigs in sequence and three sigs in sequence do occur, as has been noted, in ASL morphocherics. Two sigs and three sigs and possibly more done at the same time are also usual occurrences. Moreover a combination of sequential and simultaneous sig clustering occurs. In the group of similar signs that translate 'story', 'language', 'sentence', 'conversation' the first sig is grasp (x) which joins the double dez hands momentarily, but immediately the hands separate, closing as they move apart ($\dot{\#}$). Some signers also give the hands an oscillatory rotation at the same time, but this is a non-cheremic stylistic touch not unlike an orator's or singer's trilled [r]. A variant of the sign glossed 'pretty' (*Dictionary*, 115) has the simultaneous cluster first, the sigs circle and close, and then the outward sig is made.

A special case of sig action in time sequence is the repetition of a sig. When it occurs this is indicated in writing simply by placing a dot after the sig symbol. It is analogous to a doubled or geminated consonant in speech only in those signs with single sig. For the whole sig cluster may be repeated. But repetition of a single sig action or a sig cluster is one of the most difficult partials of sign activity to assign to an analytical level. It may be cheremic. The difference between the signs translated 'must' and 'should' (i.e. between necessity and advisability) as between those glossed 'once' and 'sometimes' also between 'back' and 'again', and between 'repeat' and 'often' is simply the difference between a sig made once and the same sig made repeatedly, usually thrice. But the repetition of a sig may also be rhetorical or stylistic. A signer may repeat a sig once, twice, or many times only for emphasis or some other meaning not easy to classify. When a signer is speaking at the same time he is signing, or when a hearing signer is interpreting what a speaker is saying the number of performances of a sig often equals the number of syllables in the word the sign translates. Repetition also has morphemic uses. The difference singular and plural signification of a sign may be simply the difference between a single sig action and its repetition. However this occurs with too few of ASL signs to define a form class or even to suggest any system of inflection of signs for number.

While repetition of a single sig may be compared with doubling of a consonant or perhaps better with lengthening a vowel, repetition of a sig cluster seems more like reduplication; the whole sign is done again, since tab and dez are just as intimately connected with sig in its repetition as in its first performance. However a special kind of repetition is unique in sign language. Interchanging action ('') is reversed repetition, a mirror-image repeat of the sign. The old dez becomes the new tab; the old tab becomes the new dez and performs the sig the other way round. In this class of sign can be seen very clearly the basic anatomical symmetry of the organism. Right and left are interchangeable in sign language as in the human and anthropoid modes of movement that form the basic material for this semiotic system. Visible anthroposemiotic systems that are derived from speech-based language take an opposite departure. Left and right may be transformed into up and down, but cannot be ignored in writing. The Greek *boustrophedon* reversed direction, but at the end of lines, not in the middle or at random the way an ASL signer can reverse hands. For the signs with interchange are only a special case of the general condition that any single dez sign can be made with either right or left hand working. Fingerspelling too is indifferent to left-right difference, and here it differs from the alphabet it encodes. The L dez looks like an upper case printed L to the signer himself if he uses his left hand, but to the addressee opposite him only if he uses his right. In short all the manual alphabet configurations, like the tab and dez cheremes of American Sign Language, are symmetrical, like printed T, A, V, X, but quite unlike B, C, D, etc.

Reversed repetition of sig action and tab and dez symmetry are here being treated morphocherically as having to do with the manner in which ASL cheremes combine into signs, and prelinguistically as having their basis in primatoid somatic structure and operation. But they also have implications with the semological system, the interrelationships of things signified in this whole semiotic. Harry Hoemann (1970) has found that deaf children perform differently from hearing children on tasks that require communicating to a partner pertinent information about right left reversal. The fact that the former group used sign language and the latter speech may not be irrelevant. The two semiotic systems, speech and sign language, use space and time differently. When speakers make language visible in writing, they use side to side and vertical displacement on a plane to render the before-to-after occurrence of language elements. Signers however use three-dimensional space to display things — usually the cheremes in a sign but sometimes the signs in a phrase — things that in speech are sequenced in the unidirectional flow of time. Signers also use time, although the medium is visual not auditory, and not side by side placement, to signal the connection of units presented.

Another morphocheremic feature is seen in the sig aspect. The manner of making a sign can vary just as a similar but non-semiotic action can, e.g. grasping. The action may be quick or lethargic, to choose opposites. It may be sharp or smooth; it may be large or small. Much of this kind of manner variation in the ASL signer's performance, like paralanguage, conveys information about the signer's own state of health, interest, age, sex, and the like (Ekman, 1969). But the parameters of this kind of action and their ranges provide vehicles for linguistic as well as paralinguistic signalling. Differences of manner may not be symptoms of an emotional state but instead may indicate a distinction between cheremes or signal a kind of relation between morphemes.

The difference between a sharp sig action and the same action without that component of intensity has not been found to make cheremic contrast in minimal pairs. Instead intensity seems to contrast with repetition of the unstressed action. Thus, e.g. the index jabs the chin ('bitter' or 'disappoint'), but it touches the chin twice lightly ('favorite'). Other contrasts in the manner of sig action seem to have more connection with syntactic structuring and with style levels. These include slowness versus faster than normal action, larger or smaller than normal movements, and probably some others not yet identified.

Juncture in ASL communication has been found to signal such messages as 'end of sentence; wait for more', 'end of sentences; your turn'; and 'end of question; begin answering'. These are terminal junctures seen as the manner in which the signer's hands change from their roles as dez or tab and dez into a posture of rest — equivalent to silence in speech exchanges. The first and second begin the same way with the hands descending relaxed from the normal signing height, but then they may either be raised again to recommence sign activity or go to full rest, usually in contact with each other, the lower resting on a convenient bodily support or furniture. To make the signal asking for response to a question, the signer's hands remain at signing height and may be more or less extended outward from the signer's own space into what may be considered the addressee's space. Nothing has been done with proxemics (Hall, 1959) in the ASL communicative encounter, but generally all observers agree that signers make more or different use of tactile signs than hearing persons in American culture, so that it is likely that their use of interpersonal space is a different system too.

Along with manner of performing sig action and juncture between rest and signing, sign and sign, and signing and rest a third associated source of signalling in sign language is regard. The head and eye action of a signer sharply differs when a question is asked and when a response is given. The cheremic content of the sign act may be identical, but the fact that the signer looks directly at the addressee to ask but to reply drops his eyes and nods the head forward were noted early. Later study of juncture features along with head-eye phenomena show that both are involved with such syntactic signalling as 'question', 'conclusion', and 'suspension'. A recent increase of interest in ASL studies has focussed much more attention on these features. Further discussion of them will be found in the chapter on morphology proper and syntax.

The most important generalization to be drawn from this examination of ASL morphocheremics is that its pattern is remarkably unsaturated. Forty or fifty aspect cheremes, and contrasts in at least three activities that occur along with cheremes, provide a great more many combinations than are used as morphemes in the language. Unlike English which has relatively few unused CVC combinations (e.g. *pat, tat, cat, bat, dat, gat, chat, jat*(?), *fat, vat, sat, shat, zat*(?), *mat, nat*, etc.), American sign language has many unused tab-dez-sig combinations. One must conclude that the language thus offers great potential for future development. Cultural, physiological, or environmental change that forced the use of a sign language on large numbers would find the ASL morphocheremic system ready for a major vocabulary expansion. (Discussion of a limited and specific vocabulary enlargement will be found in Chapter 7). This is not to say that the language is deficient in vocabulary now. Like other languages used by man it suffices for the uses to which it is put, and heretofore it has been used by only a few in academic, technological, or other activities that require extensive vocabulary. And when its users have needed a more numerous lexicon they have resorted to fingerspelling the words of English, since they are bilingual by education and since other participants in these activities are usually not signers.

But there is another cause of the apparently small vocabulary of American Sign Language. Its morphocheremic system makes a unique relation with its semantic system. While other languages package some part of meaning in a fixed discrete unit called a word and modify this by substituting different units, by attaching other units to make phrases, or by affixing still other units, American Sign Language operates with a flexible package, the sign, and it can modify its meaning over a continuum by manner changes in the sig. Thus many signs have a semantic range comparable to that of a fairly large number of related words or of a whole repertoire of phrases.

REFERENCES, CHAPTER 3

Ekman, Paul, and W. V. Friesen,
  1969 "The Repertoire of Nonverbal Behavior : Categories, Origins, Usage, and Coding", *Semiotica* 1 : 1, 49-98.
Hall, Edward T.,
  1959 *The Silent Language* (New York, Doubleday).
Hoemann, Harry W.,
  1970 "The Development of Communication Skills in Deaf and Hearing Children", Mimeographed Ph. D. Dissertation (Catholic University of America).

4

MORPHEMES — LEXICON

A complete analysis of ASL morphemics has yet to be made. Early compilers of handbooks, introducing the signs to those who do not know them, used a mixture of linguistic and semantic classifications. Thus Long (1918) arranges his sign vocabulary under these headings:

> Auxiliary Verbs
> Pronouns
> Mankind and Relationships
> Sensations, Feelings, and the Affections
> Mental Actions, Language, and the Communication of Ideas
> Motion and Action
> Occupations of Mankind
> Adjectives and Abstract Nouns
> Measurement of Time, Space, and Quantity
> Articles of Food, Fruit, etc.
> Animals
> The World and Nature
> The Deity and Religion
> Countries and Nationalities
> Prepositions and Conjunctions
> Miscellaneous
> Numbers and Counting
> Catholic Signs

The parts of speech named in this list are the classifications for the English words that gloss the signs. In random order within each group, the words are followed by descriptions of the act of making the signs to translate them; e.g. the thirteenth article in the fifth division is,

"Know, Intelligence. — Tap the forehead with the end of the hand" (Long, 1918: 56).

Recently handbook makers have alphabetized the whole list of words that gloss the signs they describe, giving up any attempt at morpheme classification as they thus avoid the problems of a meaning-based, elementary school classification. However the old method of classification persists (Roth, 1948); and Cissna, whose alphabetized *Basic Sign Language* appeared in 1963, was using at about the same time an undated mimeographed "Introduction to the Sign Language" in which the first five headings are "Pronouns", "Question Words", "Family and Relationships", "Mental", and "Emotions". It may be that grouping signs by related meanings makes them easier for a speaker of English to remember while he is in the process of learning the language, but such grouping conveys nothing about the syntax of sign language, and furthermore it leads to a serious misunderstanding of sign language as a semiotic system.

When a number of semantically related concepts are assembled in one part of a book, or when a number of objects connected with a single activity are listed, it is likely that in a sign language some of the signs naming the concepts or objects will show some morphocheric similarity. The same is true of course when rubrics for ideas and the words of a speech-based language are grouped together; e.g. a semantic as well as a morphophonic relation unites English *despair, desperate, desperation, desperately, exasperate, exasperated, exasperation,* and so on. An explanation of the close relationship is to be found in grammars that deal with the morphemics of English, and statements are usually in terms of roots, stems, and derivational affixes. However, the same or a similar relationship in the case of American Sign Language, instead of calling forth a description of ASL morphemics, has often been flourished as a proof that signs and their denotata are related iconically. Thus Myklebust writes of the "... visual-tactual ideographic images such as characterize the language of signs" (1964: 235). And Davis and Silverman, "This [sign language] is a system of conventional gestures of the hands and arms that by and large are suggestive of the shape, form, or thought which they represent" (1960: 419). These radical misconceptions of the nature of a sign language, like popular fallacies or like secondary and tertiary responses to language (Bloomfield, 1944), ought to be dispelled simply because of their inaccuracy and because as statements in textbooks of educational psychology used in the preparation of teachers of the deaf they contribute to the hostile attitude that meets deaf children

who try to continue using their natural language at school. There is
another reason for taking time to correct these misconceptions here. No
real assessment of ASL morphemics can be made as long as a belief
persists that ASL signs are natural signs instead of morphemes, are
'visual-tactual ideographic images' instead of morphocheric structures,
are suggestive shapes instead of lexemic signs.

The fact that in some cultures the forehead is associated with thought
does not make moving the hand so that the forefinger draws a small
circle on the brow the natural sign, i.e. the symptom, of thought. This
ASL sign does have semiotic features of course. Because the finger is
contiguous with the supposed site of thinking, the sign is an index.
Because motion of the finger on the forehead may be thought of as
somehow similar to the operation of thinking, the sign is an icon. Note,
however, that the term 'iconic' is misapplied to sign language as often
as the term 'non-verbal'. Because the ASL sign signifies by conventions
common to the users of this language the intensional class of 'thought',
i.e. the signer's thought, another's thought, or thought generally, the
sign is a symbol. Because the sign may be made with an emphatic manner
of moving and a facial expression which make it into a command to
the addressee to think, the sign may be a signal. But because the whole
sign (and not just the front part of the head or the finger or the movement) denotes thought in a linguistic way, the symbolic function tran-
scends the indexic, iconic, and signalic functions. With a minute altera-
tion of action, a minimal change, which is also maximal because there
is no larger jump in a lexicon than from one lexical item to another,
the sign becomes a different sign: from 'think' it becomes 'penny' with
a single touch, or 'government' if the circling precedes the touch.

This argument may be repeated many times, indeed as often as the
use of a chereme is said to be iconic or indexic only or when the pairing
of two cheremes recurs in two semantically related signs, but the conclusion will remain the same: a simplistic identification of signs similar
in appearance with general categories of meaning belongs in the folklore
and superstitions that persons of one culture use to derogate outsiders'
language.

Even if it is apparent now that an ASL morpheme is not related to
its denotatum as a fire is to heat or a blow to sound, the reader will
find manuals of American Sign Language that group signs together
because their denotata fall in the same semantic field. Signs translated
'know', 'forget', 'dream', 'smart', 'idea', 'because', 'stupid', 'misunderstand', 'remember', and 'for', as well as 'think', use forehead as tab

and touch as sig or as part of a sig combination. Some of these signs do have reference to mental operations. But the signs translating 'because' and 'for' are just as abstractly symbolic of linguistic relationship as are their glosses. Moreover the signs for 'Sweden', 'summer', 'horse', 'sick', and many others are also made with forehead tab and touch sig. This argument also can be repeated with group after semantic group of signs gathered in one or another word-sign handbook. This conclusion is also inescapable: there are signs with similar aspects which refer to semantically similar things but others with the same aspects which do not. In general, iconicity is a feature of American Sign Language, but its presence and absence as in all languages are immaterial to the semantic, morphemic, and morpheme-constituent systems.

Pronouns

One ASL form class of morphemes with semologic, syntactic, and morphocheric similarity has obvious relation to the general linguistic class of personal pronouns. In American Sign Language the signs for denoting the signer, the addressee, and a third person are indexic. Their sig is pointing, respectively, toward the signer's self, toward the addressee, and toward a real or imagined person standing so that the pointing makes an angle (either side) with the line between the first two persons. If a horizontal clock is imagined, directions for 'you' and 'I' are precisely twelve o'clock and six o'clock, but 'him' = 'that one', and 'him' = 'that other one' are less precise, about two o'clock and about ten o'clock. However, ASL sigs take place in three-dimensional space, and the signs which refer to Deity and may be rendered 'thou', 'thee', 'thy' and 'thine' point upward.[1]

The dez for all five directions, that is for all five persons, is usually index finger (G hand). Some signers use fingerspelled 'i' to render English *I* and reserve the G dez sigs for *me*. This is perhaps best regarded as borrowing, as it is seen more frequently among signers whose competence in English is greater than in sign language.

---

[1] There is considerable variation to be seen in the signing of prayers. Indeed those denominations that have a long tradition of work with the deaf have most of the characteristics of dialect centers. Their deaf congregations give continuity as does the practice of having the hearing clergy learn their signs from older colleagues and deaf parishoners instead of from the ASL community in general. The demoninational and liturgical separation of the church or mission tend to preserve these differences. The fact that the churches must communicate linguistically to fulfill their mission has also made them centers for sign language usage as contrasted with schools which may have aims and policies that discourage or forbid sign language use.

Inflexion is also a mark of this form class. When the dez is changed to flat hand (B) with palm facing in sig direction, the sememe of possession is added to that of person, thus 'your', 'my', 'his' or 'hers', and 'thy'. (Some signers make the last with the back of hand instead of the palm uppermost.) Changing the dez to fist (A) with thumb up marks another inflected form of the signs in this small but important class. The sememe added by the new component may be called 'self'. Signs with this dez do translate 'yourself', 'myself', and the rest quite satisfactorily; but some signers use the A-dez signs in contexts that suggest the added element is emphasis rather than a sememe congruent with English -*self*.

When a signer is addressing two or more persons at the same time, a second sig component is added and the dez (G or B) both points and swings in an arc to include all referents. The sign for 'they' or 'them' also swings in an inclusive arc, or uses small shakes which in effect repeat the pointing sig. The different combinations of speaker and other persons that are all denoted by English *we, us, our, ours* and *ourselves* are denoted differentially in American Sign Language. Signer and one addressee, first and second person *we* and *us,* are the denotata of a sign with K-dez and oscillating wrist action that alternately points the index in the general direction of addressee (or another person near signer) and the second finger at the signer. To include several addressees with the signer, the dez begins toward signer, swings an arc away, and returns to pointing at signer: both 'we' and 'us'. Possessive, 'our', is usually a supinating twist of upward held B dez and may begin with thumb edge contact on chest tab and finish with little finger contact. In more formal style the contact is definite and the whole arm swings out in an arc as the hand twists to finish also with definite contact. The possessive for the two-person dual 'we' is made like 'our', but the signer's eyes and face indicate the intimacy of the group.

Inanimate objects may be just as easily designated by signs that specifically symbolize them as by more general indexic signs. Objects that are present may be pointed at as persons are, but generally the direction of pointing will be lower than for persons. Another difference between third-person person and third-person object in ASL morphemics is that the former needs no overt tab; a G-hand pointed out obliquely denotes 'him' or 'her' whether the person is visible or not, but the palm-up B tab is usually used with Y dez for 'it' or 'that'. The kind of distinction a speaker of English makes by saying, 'I don't want that; I want this', will probably be shown in signing with G dez pointing at the (psychologically) nearer and the knuckles of Y dez pointing at the farther or excluded or disapproved object. If the referents were clear to the addressee, when the objects were not present to be pointed at, the two might be done with B tab; B $G_v{}^x$ 'this'; B $Y_v{}^x$ 'that'.

Form Classes

What makes one sign a noun in American Sign Language and another a verb, one an adjective and another a connective of some kind is not any regularity in morphocheric or morphemic patterning. Signs very similar in morphocheric structure may belong to different classes; e.g. 'money' and 'cook' use the same tab and dez and repeated touch sig. All that distinguishes the first (invariably a noun) from 'cook' (usually a verb) is the turning over of the dez between touches. (One who cooks is signed 'cook-er', i.e. the verb sign plus personal sign.) Again 'free' is signed by separating the crossed A_s-dez hands. But separating the crossed forefingers of G-dez hands signifies 'but'. Moreover many signs cheremically identical function either as nouns or verbs.

The identification of such morpheme classes as noun, verb, adjective, conjunction, adverb, and preposition must therefore be done with syntactic criteria. Meanwhile a few minor morpheme classes may be pointed out.

Already mentioned is the personal sign or 'body sign' as some writers term it. The signer's hands held parallel (B dez) move down along or parallel to the sides of the trunk. Used alone this sign signifies, as it indicates, 'the body', but made immediately following a sign that can have verb use it derives a personal agentive noun just as does the English suffix -er.

A large class of ASL nouns, which might be labeled by syntactic procedures, + noun, + animate, + human, subdivides into subclasses at two additional nodes. The larger number are gender-marked, but those positive at this node are either masculine or feminine, i.e. ± masculine in the logic of binary choice. The sign language nouns which do specify the sex of their referent do not actually have gender in the traditional sense, for no other features of ASL syntax must be adjusted to produce concord. Indeed, considered contrastively ASL and English nouns and pronouns are conversely opposite in these regards. The English pronouns in question differ in structure as in gender: *he* alternates with *she, him* with *her,* and *his* with *her* and *hers.* English nouns however have no paradigmatic gender system. Though *mother, sister, father, brother* show fossil morphemic difference, *girl, maid, man, boy,* like many others, are simple morphemes with no structural clues to gender. And *cousin, doctor, hairdresser,* and a long list besides are indeterminate until a speaker or writer uses a *he* or *she* to mark gender semologically.

The ASL pronouns allow no possibility of gender, but noun signs like 'girl', 'boy', 'man', 'woman', 'father', 'mother', 'aunt', 'uncle' have a morphocheric structure which makes the referent's sex an overt part of the sign. Being true indexes, ASL pronouns can relate to their deno-tatum directly, by contiguity. A signer may, in signing to a second person, point to a present third person, or to a door through which a third person has just departed. There is nothing in the sign itself to indicate that the sign is masculine or feminine and no need for it to do so. The person indicated supplies that information whether actually present or only present to the attention of both signer and addressee.

However, this is not the whole matter of ASL deictic pronouns. Just as likely of occurrence is the purely linguistic function of reference. A signer addressing a second person may refer to a third person whom the second has never encountered, e.g. a boy in his neighborhood, the signer's new niece, or any person that can be named or symbolized in the language. The signer does this with a noun sign. Immediately there-after the signer's reference to that person will be a sign that points at an angle to the line joining signer and addressee. Whether the G hand points to signer's left or right will have been determined by the signer when he named the third person; his eyes will glance to one side or the other, the same side later used for the pronoun. But now there is no one at the end of the signer's index finger for the sign to be contiguous to. The reference is therefore purely linguistic, related to the sign through ASL syntactic, semantic, and cheremic systems. Whether the sign is to be translated in English by *he* or *she, him* or *her,* cannot be now read back from a person visually indicated, but because the naming of the person originally was with a sign containing either the male morpheme (dez touches forehead) or the female morpheme (dez moves down cheek), the signer and addressee know perfectly well the sex or gender.

There is ambiguity in ASL signs for 'doctor', 'driver', 'teacher' as in the English nouns; but the easily used (prefixed) morphemes with brow or cheek tab make signs like 'policewomen' (the order of the morphemes is better suggested by the gloss 'she-cop'), 'woman driver', and 'goddess' (again, 'she-god').

The nature of ASL person determination, it will be noticed, like the cheremic features of the language generally, makes no distinction of

left and right. Signer and addressee establish a line; points off the line
are for third persons, for adjuncts to a central message, or for objects.
But if 'he' is to the signer's left, the same 'he' must be to addressee's
right and vice versa. This may be one of the factors accounting for the
different success with which speaking children and signing children
communicate information about rotationally transformed and reflec-
tionally transformed pictures (Hoemann, 1970).

Lexicon

There is no way to compare the lexicon of American Sign Language
and the lexicon of English directly, and there would be little value in
such a comparison if it could be made. The third edition of Webster's
New International Dictionary advertises, '450,000 entries'. The total
number of all ASL signs recorded in all the handbooks and dictionaries
in print cannot be much above four thousand. Even were the proportion
only one hundred to one, the operation of mapping almost half a million
words onto a few thousand signs is more than prohibitively arduous,
worse than futile, it is in fact impossible. Because American Sign Language is the medium of communication used by a community of people
(or a social group or a subculture), anything expressible in another
language can be expressed in it. Translation however is not a simple
matter of substituting a sign for a word. The English word *incompatibility*
may be rendered with a sequence of two signs, 'get along' 'nothing';
but the interpreter must decompose the whole structure in which the
word appears as well as the word and recompose a sign sentence which
will represent the significance of the source sentence. Thus if 450,000
English words and four thousand signs were to be put into parallel
columns or lists, the operation of mapping one set onto or into the
other could still not be performed. A simple example of mapping is the
relation of letters and numbers on a telephone dial. If the letter is A
or B or C, all three are equivalent, as far as dialing is concerned, to
the numeral '2'. All three map into '2'. But if '2' is given, there is no
way to know which letter may be behind it, and the operation of mapping
from numeral to letter cannot be performed.

At first sight, word-to-sign mapping seems to be feasible. The English
words *have, possess,* and *own* all map into the sign made by bending
the hand so that the fingertips touch the chest; but an interpreter seeing
the sign could not determine without more context which word to choose.
Thus going from *have, possess,* or *own* to the sign seems to be one-way

mapping as in the telephone dial example. However it is not, because the English word *have* also has another use that requires a different sign, the hand shaken perpendicularly to the wrist. Since the word *have* alone does not indicate which of the two signs is to be selected (any more than '22' in a telephone number indicates whether the exchange is BAker or CAmbridge), there is no possibility of mapping *have* into signs. Since this is so and since the signs described cannot be mapped into words either, the vocabulary lists of American Sign Language and English are not functions of each other.

Of course the same statement can be made about the lexicons of any pair of languages, and the same proofs, that one set of words cannot be mapped into another, work for any pair of languages also. It is a statement worth emphasizing about sign language, however, because, one, it is believed by many persons that the signs of American Sign Language are English words coded as gestures, and, two, there is a way of rendering English sentences by assuming a convention in which words and signs are so related — the latter procedure is 'signed English' and not American Sign Language.

What is peculiar about the lexicon of American Sign Language is the way signs retain their general semantic significance while freely moving from one to another specific grammatical category. Thus one sign, C-tab, M-dez, not only has prepositional use, by which it translates English *in* but also functions as a verb with senses like 'include' and 'put in' and as an adjective, 'inside', and as an adverb. Other signs that are found in English-Sign handbooks as equivalents of adjectives are adjectival only in certain uses and have verb force that the bilingual dictionary cannot show because English adjectives are not verbs also. Consequently the only useful way to deal with the entire lexicon of American Sign Language is in connection with the syntactic structures of that language along with the semological patterns that syntax and signs as lexical items produce.

One way of considering the lexicon in part is to begin with a list of signs in the order of their frequency of use. Unfortunately no such list has been made and compiling a corpus and making a frequency count is not easily done although it is possible to reduce signs to cheremic symbols. Lacking a list of sign frequencies, it is possible with caution to use a list of English words of high frequency and to observe the sign lexicon contrastively. The most frequently used word in English is *the*, and the second, *of*. (The frequencies and rank orders used here are those obtained from George K. Monroe's 285,062 word corpus of the

Brown University Standard Corpus as presented in William Card's and Virginia McDavid's "English Words of Very High Frequency" in *College English* 27:8 [1966], 596-604). Immediately a difference of considerable importance is apparent. American Sign Language does not have articles. There is no sign to translate *of* either. To one who knows no grammar but English grammar, these two words are so frequent and so prominent in grammar that a language without direct literal translations for them must seem less than grammatical. But in fact many languages are like sign language and unlike English in this respect, having no definite article and no word or particle to translate every occurrence of the word *of*. One of the first lessons of linguistics is that believing one's native grammar to be universal grammar is provincial superstition. Semiotics has something to add here as well. Both *the* and *of* are closely associated in English with the structure of the noun phrase, or of nominals, or of nominal fields — those stretches of syntax whose function is to denote something that will by them be differentiated from all the things that it is not. But there are usually other ways of denoting or denominating the same thing in one language and always other ways of denoting it in another language; e.g. if someone says in giving directions: 'keep on to the end of the road', it might be paraphrased, 'continue to the road end', or 'go on till the road ends'. One translation of this in American Sign Language, with the sequence of signs rendered here by their usual glosses, might be, 'road' 'end'. In English the choice and use of *the* and *of* depend on numerous semantic features, among them definite, generic, aggregate, common, count (Chafe, 1970). Some of these features are made visible or are unnecessary to specify because the sign itself is visible not just as a spoken morpheme is audible but also visible with all its aspects. Therefore the latent iconic or indexic functions of the aspects can participate in the semiotic ensemble. In the translation the sign 'end' is symbolic but also its sig puts its dez in contiguity with the just presented dez of 'road' so that a part of the sign 'end' acts as index to the sign 'road'. Moreover, the placement of the hands in the two signs is iconic as well. The parallel dez hands of 'road' resemble the sides of a road while the perpendicular hand of 'end' is similar to a barrier. This kind of indexic and iconic obligato on the main symbolic theme of signs in syntactic arrangement may be no less complex than the semantic features and the rules for generating English noun phrases from them. But the fact that the two languages accomplish the same communicative function by different means is no grounds for calling one grammatical and the other not.

And is the third most frequent word in English. It has a literal equivalent in American Sign Language as it has in most languages. However the sign 'and' is by no means congruent with English *and*. Two words in English must have *and* between them if their correlation is the conjunctive one. The ASL rule is diametrically opposite; e.g. *father and mother* but 'father' 'mother'; *eat and run* but 'eat' 'run'; or *red and yellow* but 'red' 'yellow'. As a sign of American Sign Language 'and' has a curious status. (It is made in zero tab by drawing the 5-dez horizontally parallel to the chest as it closes to pointed M.) It is the only sign allowed in pure fingerspelling; i.e. when fingerspelling is used without signs, as some think it must be so that deaf users will acquire correct English. No abbreviations of fully spelled English words are permitted except this one; therefore it may be considered a manually coded typographic symbol, '&', just as letters are. Its essentially foreign nature in ASL structure is also indicated by its absence from the commonest conjunction correlations and by its frequent appearance when the structure of English sentences is encoded into signs as surrogates for words.

The fourth English word in rank order is *to*. It can be translated by a sign, but again it will often be absent from translations of English structures that use it. It also translates 'up to', 'until', and 'at', but a great many English correlations in which it is the correlator, e.g. *speak to me,* use no sign as correlator when translated into American Sign Language. Again the explanation is afforded by semiotics. A correlation in which the first thing to be correlated is directed toward the second correlatum does not need an explicit correlator because the sign which contains the first correlatum usually has a sig which have can indexic force. And not only is the indexic function latent in many ASL sigs, making overt prepositions unnecessary, but also it is common to see a signer use the sign glossed 'to' in translating both words of English expressions like *go to, went to,* and *gone to.* One might say that the sign is a transitive verb of motion which takes a noun naming a location as direct object.

The next word in order is *a,* the preconsonantal indefinite article, which like the definite article has no representation in the ASL lexicon.

The word *in,* sixth in rank order (and appearing 6,160 times in a 285,000 word corpus) has already been noted in connection with the sign which translates it as well as *include, put in, insert,* and the like.

The seventh word *is,* shows a sharp drop in frequency of occurrence from the first five, being used only little more than half as often as *in* and one-sixth as often as *the* (respectively: 3,417; 6,160; 20,172). It also marks another region where English and American Sign Language have little common ground, for the latter is one of many languages without the copula. What an English grammar calls adjectives and adverbs are used with verb force by signers. Therefore there are no signs for *is* (rank order 6) *was* (13), *be* (15), *are* (19), *were* (37), *been* (43), *being* (118). However, there are signs for all of these in what is often referred to as sign language but which is more accurately called signed English, i.e. English sentences coded for a deaf addressee or audience by substituting signs for words. Because the ASL sign glossed 'true', 'real', 'exist', etc. has some semantic relation to *be,* the sign is used as the basis for a whole paradigm of signs which are currently being used in signed English. An older prescription gave the sig for 'true' as an upward thrust while the G-dez moved outward from the lips and the sig for 'be' or 'is' as a straight or slightly downward sig. Those who see in signed English a way of helping deaf pupils achieve competence in English keep the tab and sig the same for these copula signs: B-dez 'be', B-G-dez 'being', W-dez 'was', 'were' (with added differentia), R-dez 'are'. The use of these signs to translate the forms of English *be* is an alternative to fingerspelling these words. Both practices have their advocates and opponents.

The eighth word in English rank order of frequency is the multipurpose *that,* pronoun, demonstrative adjective, determiner, and clause introducer. The sign made by thrusting the fist into the palm — actually the thumb and little finger are out, so dez is Y — translates *that* in its pronoun uses; i.e. the sign in ASL sentences has pronoun force. But it is also used in signed English to encode any occurrence of *that.* Shifting the point of view from lexicon to syntax, there is considerable difference in the ways English and American Sign Language users produce result and relative clauses.

The English word *for* (ninth in rank order) translates the French *pour* in most instances, and it is well documented that Épée invented a sign to translate the latter (1776; Stokoe, 1960: 11-12). The sign remains in American Sign Language having survived importation of the older sign language to America. It is an integral part of the ASL system and not just a means of translating *for* in signed English, although it was originally one of Épée's *signes méthodiques* or 'signed French'. Evidence for this is seen in the idiomatic use of the sign once or more repeated with a questioning facial expression to ask 'What's the meaning of that?' or 'What did you do that for?'

TABLE I

1 [the]	32 they	63 into	94 those
2 [of]	33 you	64 up	95 through
3 and	34 had	65 our	96 each
4 to	35 we	66 first	97 because
5 [a]	36 all	67 two	98 my
6 in	37 [were]	68 your	99 *year*
7 [is]	38 their	69 *time*	100 [*state*]
8 that	39 would	70 most	101 before
9 for	40 who	71 them	102 *people*
10 it	41 more	72 do	103 like
11 with	42 can	73 she	104 how
12 as	43 [been]	74 over	105 much
13 [was]	44 *new*	75 also	106 *way*
14 on	45 there	76 [such]	107 where
15 [be]	46 if	77 any	108 *make*
16 he	47 when	78 many	109 [just]
17 by	48 [its]	79 then	110 [*well*]
18 this	49 than	80 could	111 very
19 [are]	50 no	81 after	112 under
20 at	51 *said*	82 now	113 *day*
21 his	52 so	83 last	114 *work*
22 from	53 only	84 *years*	115 *use*
23 have	54 other	85 *made*	116 three
24 or	55 may	86 even	117 too
25 not	56 some	87 must	118 [being]
26 but	57 what	88 *world*	119 own
27 which	58 these	89 *good*	120 since
28 [an]	59 him	90 *man*	121 still
29 will	60 out	91 should	122 *used*
30 has	61 her	92 *Mrs.*	
31 one	62 about	93 *Mr.*	

A general view of this part of the lexicon of English in comparison with American Sign Language may be more revealing than an item by item comparison. One hundred and six of the 122 most frequent words in English have close or exact sign equivalents. Table I lists all of them in rank order. The 16 words for which there is no sign translation are shown in brackets. The words in italics are the 20 content words not included in the 102 function words discussed above. The 16 words in brackets, which have no sign language equivalents may be classified in a small number of grammatical categories as Table II shows. Sign language, as the last line in Table II indicates, belongs to that large class of languages that do not have the copula. Neither does it have the same system of determiners that English possesses. These two contrasts in grammatical system cause interference, i.e. numerous errors made in writing and speaking English by signers who have not completely learned the system of English. However the contrastive information to be gained from the non-pairing of these few words with signs is only a small part of what can be revealed by the mapping of 90 out of 102 English function words into signs.

TABLE II

1	preposition	*of*
2	content words	*state, well*
2	adverbials	*such, just*
4	articles/determiners	*the, a, an, its*
7	forms of copula	*is, was, be, are, were, been, being*

Twenty words of very high frequency are found in the classes Card and McDavid call determiners and determiners/pronominals. Sixteen of these words have sign translations: *their, no, our, your, my, that, this, his, all, some, these, her, any, those, each, much*. All the signs translating these words may be used before noun signs and some of them may be used as pronouns. Thus, while the absence of signs for *the, a, an*, and *its* argue an important difference between sign language and English nominal field structure, the presence of sixteen signs in sign language that equal the twenty most frequent English words with this grammatical function shows a substantial similarity here between English and sign syntax.

In the case of prepositions and prepositions/adverbials again it is the first, the most frequent word, *of*, that is not found in sign language. The other sixteen all gloss signs in frequent use: *for, with, at, from, into, like, to, in, on, by, out, about, up, over, through, under*. The grammatical and semological systems of English and signs are closely related by this 16-to-17 mapping. Spatial, directional, inclusional, similar, purposive, and agentive relationships are expressible in both languages of course; but the evidence from the words of very high frequency and their sign equivalents is that such relationships are easily translatable. However the absence of a sign for *of* points to a most important difference in the syntactic-semantic functioning of the two languages. There is a well defined problem for further investigation in just this divergence.

One word of caution is in order, however. Although all ten words in the class that Card and McDavid call prepositions/adverbials have matching signs, their use in sign language cannot be predicted from their occurrence in English. Some verb-particle combinations take a single sign translation, others need a verb-sign, adverbial-sign combination.

But the adverbial sign is not invariably the gloss of the English adverbial. Conversely a single verb in English may require translation by a verb-adverb sign combination.

Eight personal pronouns stand high on the list of the 122 most frequent words in the Monroe portion of the Brown Standard Corpus, from *it*, rank order 10, to *she*, rank order 73. The words between in order are *he, they, you, we, him,* and *them*. Three points at which English and sign language grammar contrast appear when the pronouns are examined. The first is that sign language does not exhibit grammatical gender. No form changes in sign verbs are required when subjects vary over the range of masculine, feminine, neuter, common, and plural pronouns. Since English does have alternative verb forms that must be used with gender-marked and unmarked subject nominal fields, errors in subject-verb concord may arise when the bilingual person thinks in signs and writes or speaks in English.

The second contrast that appears when comparing the pronoun lists of the two languages does not often lead to grammatical interference but may cause a translator difficulty at times. English pronouns belong to a still much inflected set, though the pronoun system of other Indo-European languages shows how much more elaborate such things have been. Sign language pronouns have but two cases, absolute and possessive. They do distinguish persons, first, second, and third, and may add fourth and fifth (Stokoe, 1965: 281). They also distinguish singular and plural in all three persons, while modern English has only *you* for both numbers. These differences in the pronoun systems of American Sign Language and English make a two-way mapping impossible. The systems are not congruent. A simplified symbolic representation of pronoun signs will allow the differences to be displayed.

(Table III). In the table a circle represents a signer in plan view. A line at the top of a circle indicates a sign pointing toward addressee, at the bottom pointing toward signer's self, ond obliquely, pointing toward a third person. Plural, more than one person in any of the three categories, can be treated as an additional morpheme at this point (though not often elsewhere) in sign language grammar. Plural is shown in Table III variously, by a bent line (for a sweeping, inclusive motion) or by lines closes together (for repeated pointing). Dots inside a circle represent pointing downward used to indicate objects as distinguished from persons. As the table shows, the English-Sign and Sign-English relations of these similar yet contrasting pronoun systems are not semmetrical.

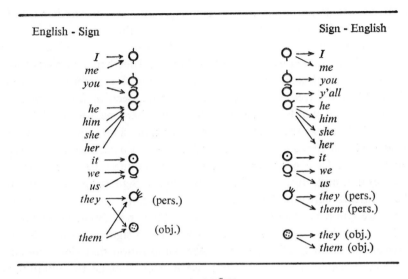

English - Sign

Sign - English

TABLE III

The third point of contrast in English and sign language pronouns has to do directly with frequency of occurrence. It is very likely that sign pronouns would show a much lower frequency if a corpus were to be compiled of ordinary conversation. This is because sign language, unlike English, often contains the subject or object reference, or more rarely both, implicitly in verb signs (Stokoe, 1965: 281-282).

The correlatives, *and, or, but,* are fully and congruently represented in sign language by three unequivocal signs whose frequency is undoubtedly high. The same is true of the relative/interrogative words and signs: *which, who, what, how,* and *where. Why* would surely be added if the corpus included much conversation particularly in learning situations.

In the Card-McDavid classification of numerative adjectivals only *such* has no sign equivalent in common use. *One, more, other, first, two, most, many, last, three, own* all have sign translations. The last word, *own,* as in 'my own idea' does not have a separate sign from *my;* but if it is understood as emphatic in English, there is a distinction too between that construction and 'my idea' in sign language. Of more interest is the absence of a sign for *such.* Presumably constructions such as the following must be handled quite differently in sign language: (a) *Such things are not worth bothering about;* (b) *It was such a childish joke that I laughed;* and (c) *I won't accept any such excuses.* Nevertheless such statements are made in sign language, and here is another clearly defined area for investigation of the syntax of that language.

The six subordinators, *if, when, after, because, before,* and *since,* are also words with unequivocal sign translations. Together the classes Card and McDavid call auxiliaries and modals account for almost ten percent of the 122 most frequent words. There are eighteen of them and only twenty content words in the list. However when the forms of *be* are removed, because the sign language grammar does not contain the copula, eleven remain: *have, has, had, do, will, would, can, may, could, must, should.* Like pronouns auxiliary verbs connect to a great many structural ramifications. And like the English-Sign pronoun relations, the contrasts between these eleven words and the signs that translate them are complex. The question of *have*/'have' was discussed above.

The word *do* as 'act' has a sign, but use of this sign as auxiliary is also interference from English patterns. Any supposition that sign language is grammatically impoverished because it cannot make the ubiquitous question and negative transformations with *do* and *did* overlooks the fact that Chaucer did quite well grammatically without them. Sign language does use *do* as a general or indefinite verb but not as emphatic or transposing auxiliary.

In the modals too, word and sign pairings suggest more pattern similarity than actually exists. Will and would are translated by the same sign. Again in translating from signs to English the English distinction has to be observed. Likewise *can* and *could* map into one sign with the burden on the translator of determining which English word to go to from the one sign. *Must* and *should* are related in a different way. Their sign translations are two forms of the same sign, differing only in that the sig (significant motion) for 'must' is a sharp movement down and for 'should' is the same motion rapidly repeated. The meaning of this 'should' is of course the 'ought to' sense differentiated from the subjunctive past of shall. For example, the following sentence is translatable sign-for-word: *If you must have foreign language; you should take Russian.*

The five miscellaneous words of the Card and McDavid grammatical classification show also miscellaneous relations of word to sign. *As* has a sign not easily distinguished from the sign 'like'. *Not* has several signs; that is, negative ideas are not expressed in a parallel way in English and sign language. *There* in signs is an adverb of place not an expletive; again this marks a considerable syntactic contrast between English and sign language. *Than* has a sign equivalent, and comparisons, by and large, are patterns similar in the two languages. *So* as a result introducing word has a sign equivalent, but *so* modifying a sentence element so as to require a result clause, or introducing an infinitive as in this sentence, is not a part of sign language.

To sum up, sign language has about one sign to each one hundred and fifty in English when total vocabularies are compared. However when the 122 most frequently used words of English are listed, signs in common use can be found for 106 of them. In the list of 122, 102 are function words; and signs map into 90 of them.

REFERENCES, CHAPTER 4

Bloomfield, Leonard,
    1944 "Secondary and Tertiary Responses to Language", *Lg.* 20, 45-55.
Card, William, and Virginia McDavid,
    1966 "English Words of Very High Frequency", *College English* 27:8, 596-604.
Chafe, Wallace L.,
    1970 *Meaning and the Structure of Language* (Chicago, University of Chicago Press).
Cissna, Roy L.,
    1963 *Basic Sign Language* (Jefferson City, Mo., Missouri Baptist Press).
    N.d. *Introduction to Sign Language* (Jefferson City, Mo., Missouri Baptist Convention).
Davis, Hallowell, and S. R. Silverman,
    1960 *Hearing and Deafness* (New York, Holt).
Épée, Charles Michel de l',
    1776 *Institution des sourds-muets* (Paris).
Hoemann, Harry W.,
    1970 "The Development of Communication Skills in Deaf and Hearing Children", Mimeographed Ph.D. Dissertation (Catholic University of America).
Long, J. Schuyler,
    1918 *The Sign Language: A Manual of Signs* (Council Bluffs, Iowa) (1962 reprint, Washington, D.C., Gallaudet College).
Myklebust, Helmer R.,
    1964 *The Psychology of Deafness* (New York, Grune and Stratton).
Roth, Stanley D.,
    1948 *A Book of Basic Signs Used by the Deaf* (Fulton, Mo., Missouri School for the Deaf).
Stokoe, William C., Jr.,
    1970 "CAL Conference on Sign Language", *The Linguistic Reporter* 12, 5-8.

5

SYNTAX

In explanation of the theory of relativity, someone wrote a long time ago that if the universe were imagined to be a flat sheet of paper, one crease in the paper would affect everything in the universe — presumably a multitude of lines on the paper. Of course drawing one more line on the paper has quite an effect too, for complete description of every line ought then to be revised to include its relation to the new line. However, the two cases differ. The geometry of Euclid is perfectly adequate to describe lines on a plane surface in such a way that one new line or many would offer no difficulties and the science of line description would remain undisturbed. But nothing in that science of plane figures and surfaces would do to cope with a distortion of the plane such as a crease in the paper would make. The science of description needs drastic revision in that case.

And this affords a close analogy to the science of language description. Most linguists are confident that the discovery of a new, i.e. hitherto unknown, language can offer no difficulties. All of the thousands of languages known to modern science are ultimately transposable as it were to lines on the same plane surface. They are used by groups of human beings. They have vocal sounds as their physical manifestation. They assemble individual sounds in a systematic, recurring, way. They fit such assemblies together. They have aspects and variously abstracted bits of the experience of their users as their semantic substance. Any new language added to them can be described in precisely the same way as all the rest are described. The details of its description must differ, otherwise it would not be another language; but the general outline must be the same, otherwise it would not be a language.

A sign language added to the languages of the world, however, is not like an added line but like a crease in the smooth surface of language science. It is used by groups of human beings. The elements of its physical manifestation are assembled in a recurrent, systematic way. It has a system to fit such assemblies together. It too has aspects and variously abstracted bits of its users' experience for its semantic substance. But the one point of difference, it has visible actions as its physical manifestation, amounts to a distortion of the smooth surface of vocal data that language science takes for its own.

The expedients adopted to deal with this distortion reveal something of the progress of language science. The Abbé de l'Épée during the Enlightenment simply distinguished between natural and methodical sign languages. If the deaf who used sign language perforce were to attain to the spiritual and intellectual heights of the age, they needed the full semantic and syntactic range of the French language; so Épée invented on a grand scale signs, visible actions, that by convention represented the morphemes of French, to supplement the morphemes of natural signing and so to bring the visual language closer to the semantic range of the *parole et langue* of French culture.

Later, when the attention of philologists was focussed on those sound correspondences that show the relation of Indo-European languages to each other and to a common tongue of great antiquity, the existence of a sign language was completely forgotten. Almost equally neglected were the languages of the world not related to the classical languages of Europe and of India. Or so it seemed to American anthropologists who sought to describe in detail the languages used by American Indians. One of them, Garrick Mallery (1881), did devote full attention to a sign language, the sign-talk of the Plains; but he describes it by telling how the signer signals words of English, or more properly the meanings of the words; and his further exploration of other sign languages leads him to the conclusion that there is but one sign language, universal, human, natural. Somehow, Mallery seems to say, signing escaped when the tongues of man were confounded at the Tower of Babel.

When American anthropological linguistics came into its majority, it swung the balance of language study from historical-comparative to descriptive-systematic, but this discipline had as little to do with sign language as had comparative philology. Language was a system of vocal symbols in that view, and sign language therefore had to be dependent on some speech, derived from some other language; or, since writing is a visual symbol system representing vocal or morphemic elements of language, sign languages might be made of symbols of symbols of symbols.

The present writer in 1960 adopted the strategy of analyzing the visual manifestation of sign language exactly as one would go about analysis of speech in an unknown language. Minimal pairs establish cheremes, /kériyms/, manifested by allochers as phonemes are by allophones. Graphic symbols for each chereme make it possible to write a sign language, that is to represent cheremically the ultimate constituents of stretches of signing; but treating sign language thus gives no assurance that in all other respects save the chereme-morpheme difference it is therefore system congruent with spoken languages.

The recent article of belief that a language is a well-defined system which can be completely described by a finite set of rules applied with mathematical rigor continues to keep sign language out of the general consideration of language and languages. In terms of the opening analogy, the theory of linear generation of syntactic structures seems to be saying that all language is or can be represented as on a plane surface. And indeed transformation is often first taught and most easily understood in principle by considering how the figures of plane geometry may be transformed by rotation and the like, keeping certain qualities invariant, or how they may be transformed into other shapes keeping surface invariant.

Again the presence of sign language tests the rule, *exceptio regulum probat*. In this case the rule is the whole set of rules that begins with S, includes the depth-to-surface transformations for a particular language, and ends with specification of all the features of the sounds needed to produce that S in speech. Sign language is the exception that tests these rules and finds them wanting. The obvious incongruity between a sign language and languages on the generative-transformational plane is that it issues in visible actions instead of in speech. Advocates of that theory of grammar specification suggest that a slight modification is in order: replace the phonological component of the rule set with a set of rules to manifest the syntactic-semantic input to them as visible action. There are several lines of argument to show that this adjustment is not sufficient, but they all lead back to the same place: sign language syntax cannot be described by the usual syntactic generation rules. Or to put it differently, generative-transformational grammarians have no more justification for replacing the phonological component with a cherological one than the present writer had for assuming that once cheremes had been described the morphology and semology of sign language would be found to lie on the same plane as those systems in other languages. What is needed is a closer look at the difference made in various linguistic theories when sign language is included in their universe of discourse.

Seven theoretical substructures or conceptual platforms are presently available for launching deep explorations into sign language. These are, in approximately the order of their appearance, traditional, structural, tagmemic, stratificational, correlational, generative, and operational. Each of these more or less completely articulated theories of language can illuminate certain features of sign language structure and system; but because a theoretical model is an instrument of analysis, each may through instrumental error inherent in it obscure other features. Certainly examining American Sign Language in the light of each theory reveals interesting facets of the theory and eventually the use of different theoretical approaches may make the nature of sign language clearer.

Traditional

There are many traditions of language study, but following the lead of Gleason (1965) we may take two of these as together forming the tradition usually referred to. The two are the scholarly-philological tradition and the school treatment. The former carries on the venerable Sanskrit, classical, and Germanic traditions of grammatical study. The latter is usually prescriptive, confusing rhetoric and semantics and a kind of logic with grammar, often with the addition of etiquette and social usage. Although one is venerated and the other may be practical, there is little interest in either tradition today among practicing linguists.

School grammar, normative, authoritarian, and often productive of absurdity as well as rebellion, is however still very much alive in sign language handbooks, manuals showing how to 'make the sign' for this idea or that word. Part of this tradition too is the collection of texts, language outlines, keys, methods, and other teaching materials used on deaf children being taught English. These may be supposed to have some effect on the sign language of persons on whom they are imposed; and since the bias in this tradition has always been anti-intellectual, simplistic, and monovalued (Gleason, 1965: 3-10), the effect of following it to write a sign language manual is usually to present sign language as a last resort, a forced choice, a necessary evil, a desperate expedient, as something a clergyman or a parole officer might have to resort to for communication with those deaf persons who have not learned to speak and to read lips. Of course evidence from the United Kingdom (Lewis, 1968) and Finland (Pesonen, 1968), two nations whose whole educational effort for the deaf is directed at speech production and speechreading, shows such communication as less than ten percent effective. Sign language is not, however, the desperate expedient a treatment of it in the school grammar tradition might make it seem. It is instead the first and only language with symbols immediately accessible to persons born without hearing or deafened early in life (Cicourel and Boese, 1971). Even if valid linguistic information about sign language were to be presented in school-grammar format in order to win an entry into classrooms, it might not gain a hearing. The effect could be like that of expounding the theory of evolution in the local dialect of a fundamentalist community.

The scholarly tradition should be able to make a greater contribution to the understanding of sign language and its place in human history and affairs as well as in the whole semiotic complex of mankind. By treating the language with the same critical and humanistic care that has been bestowed on classical, hebraic, and modern languages of high prestige, the scholar-grammarian might raise sign language in the estimation of its users and gain it and them a more favorable attention from others. However it is the nature of a tradition to retain more than it adopts and discards. The difficulty already experienced of fitting the classical categories and terminology to the less inflected languages of Europe and America will be magnified by applying them to a sign language, not only less inflected than English but of radically different structure throughout its grammar. Even were there today a receptive audience for a scholarly traditional treatment of sign language grammar and accidence, it would probably fail of its purpose; exposing the still greater difference of its structure from Latin, such a grammar might lower the language and its users in the esteem of the philologist, if he happens to be lover of the inflected and derived word.

Structural

The structuralist view of language is less than a unified vision at present. One line on it may be established, not terminated, by two points, Bloomfield's "Postulates for a Science of Language" (1926), and Trager's "Linguistics is Linguistics" (1963). The same line gave the basis or bias for the earliest linguistic treatments of a sign language (West, 1960; Stokoe, 1960; 1965). In essence a structuralist view sees the semology (where the language interpenetrates the lives of its users) as explainable only by full analysis of the morphological units, structures, and system, and these only by a full analysis of the phonology.

As a theory it seems both consistent and ambitious enough, and the criticisms of it by proponents of other theories and by philosophers of science need not be reviewed here. As a model for the analysis of a sign language it requires beginning with well defined data and a careful consideration of the physical manifestation, i.e. cherology rather than phonology here. It provides the necessary conceptual machinery in its allo- and -eme concepts for dealing with the substance of sign language activity by establishing the inventory of the visual structure points, the diacritics of their relations, and their distribution in the system. More than this, it provides the terminology for description. Thus the important differences between a sign language proper like American Sign Language and a semiotically diverse system like fingerspelling can be put clearly in the terms and concepts of structural linguistics. Moreover other sign languages, other manual alphabetical systems, and even non-verbal behavior that uses the same physiological apparatus and manifestations are accessible to structural analysis that begins with the sames and differents observable in the acts of signing.

Essentially such acts are like other such acts in whole or in part, and by the use of structural theory the analyst of a sign language sets out to identify ever more accurately the visually distinctive features on which similarities and differences are determined. Again this theory is not limited to any particular sign language as long as that involves the signer's hands and body. Certain axes around which variation occurs are by now obvious. Sign activity varies in place, so that location somehow defined is significant. Configurations, i.e. visually distinct appearances of the hand or hands are exploited in all semiotic systems involving the hands, so that they too are significant. Finally, the action of the hand or hands may be simple or complex and may vary in numerous ways, so that action too is significant.

Still following the structural model, this kind of information may be codified as an inventory of the tab, dez, and sig cheremes of American Sign Language. Equally it may be used to compare and contrast two sign languages or dialects with minute accuracy or to express the difference between linguistic and paralinguistic function: the aspects of two signers' performance may differ allocherically, i.e. be part of the same sign having the same denotatum, but also differ in ways that another signer reads as difference in the personalities, attitudes, or circumstances of the two. In short, it is hard to conceive of a linguistic treatment of sign language that could dispense with the tab, dez, and sig aspect cheremes derived from structural theory.

Where the theory appears to be less helpful is in the description of morpheme classes and combinations, in explanation of sign syntactic structures. This may be the failure of the analyst or the impenetrability of the material or both and not the fault of the theory. The best forms of structuralist theory provide for a major difference in phoneme types, segmental vs. supersegmental. Morphemes are likewise seen opposed, and only the addition of a suprasegmental morpheme to the segmental can make a complete word with grammatical and phonetic as well as lexical properties. The analogy may not be close, but if one thinks of the major difference between electrical circuit components and the electric current flowing in them it is easy to see how important other then segmental elements are in this theory.

Unfortunately no satisfactory analysis has been made of elements in American Sign Language which correspond to pitch, stress, and juncture phonemes still less of morphemes comparable to superfixes. Certain manners of sign activity seem to have at least physiological similarity to supersegmentals, but degrees of force in signing do not pattern like stress differences, being largely non-cheremic. Juncture phenomena have been studied (Covington, in Stokoe, 1965: 275), but the simplest way to incorporate the ASL signals for 'end of message', 'reply to my query', and 'wait for more' into a description of the language is to make them a small class of morphemes composed as other morphemes in the language are of tab, dez, and sig.

But such treatment is not in keeping with the opposition of segmental and suprasegmental morphemes of the theory. In American Sign Language another kind of activity seems to be more closely analogous to the signalling function of pitch, stress, and juncture. This is facial activity, so called, though it comprehends more than the facial features; in fact all the signer's body not involved directly in the manual chereme production may be so considered. What the signer's face and body do while the hands are signing cannot be separated from significant sign activity. Like suprasegmental phenomena it is both an inevitable accompaniment to the stuff commonly thought of as the separable bits of language and it is capable too of significant variation. The difficulty in utilizing all this in the structural model is that unlike stress, pitch, and juncture, this facial component of signing can occur alone so that a description of sign language may be quite different from a structural description of some other language.

Of course structural theory makes no requirement of analogy. What may ultimately be found to be the structure of American Sign Language may very well require a description quite unlike structural grammars of other languages. Meanwhile there are other theoretical approaches to sign language to be considered.

Tagmemic

The proper title of the next theory of language which might be used to consider sign language shows that it is more than a linguistic theory: *Language in Relation to a Unified Theory of the Structure of Human Behavior* (Pike, 1954, 1955, 1960). Like all system builders its originator may have ideas of a special order of magnitude. It is the writer's experience that the system seems pellucid and practical when expounded by Pike himself but no more than an ordinary theory when applied by his followers or tried by an apprentice hand. Particle, wave, and field make excellent terms to use both of language organization and of human behavior generally. Like other trilogs, unit, profile, system, or isolate, set, pattern, they can be applied over and over again. The particles first discerned become the fields of a new look with higher power and more resolution in the instrument. It is quite possible that a use of the tagmemic approach by an investigator of Pike's perspicacity might discover much worth knowing about sign language; e.g. particles might be discovered at some spatial or behavioral distance from the phenomena commonly supposed to compose a sign language form. As with other theories, this one will be most successful when applied by one who has a native speaker's knowledge of sign language.

Yet it is presumably from this theoretical platform that Pike performs his 'monolingual demonstration' which many linguists have witnessed. He "works with an informant unknown to him ... and whose language he does not know. The informant may use only his native language and Professor Pike uses Mixtec, a Mexican Indian language. Without the use of English, and with only a few 'props' (such as a rock, a leaf, a stick), he conducts an introductory linguistic exploration of the informant's language" (Program, 1967). This demonstration is more than an introductory linguistic exploration, because to make it the explorer must communicate with his informant. This communication itself is in the present context as interesting as the information it elicits about the informant's language.

It proceeds haltingly, of necessity. The explorer begins with a greeting in Mixtec; then the informant may or may not respond with a greeting in his own language. Most of the time not speech but the explorer's actions elicit the informant's vocal response. He holds out a stone, adds another to it, holds a stick, breaks it, walks away, sits down, offers and withdraws a prop. In short, the communication proceeds in a mixture of Mixtec, language X, and what ever since 1492 has been erroneously labeled 'sign language'. Instead of trading iron pots and beads for furs and feathers, the explorer here is trading Mixtec and pantomime, vocal noise and human action, for utterances in language X. The fundamental and necessary conditions for the exchange are not just two languages and two monolinguals. Also necessary are the functional hearing of both participants and the characteristic in some cultures at least) of responding with speech to speech, with speech to gesture, and with speech to objects in the environment. When the former of these conditions is not met, the latter may be absent also.

Some of the basic nature of communication is changed when it does not operate in the normal channels of hearing and speech. When signing becomes something more than an admittedly clumsy *ad hoc* link between speakers quite ignorant of each others language, when sign language with its own syntax and lexicon becomes the medium of communication, then communicative behavior is structured so differently that the validity of tagmemic theory is open to question. To be sure physical laws are stated with the proviso 'under standard conditions', and any theory of language may provide also normal sensory functioning in order to attain to the generality desired; but human beings seem to be somewhat more than the sum of their sense impressions and human communication more than what is possible and common to those in the great majority who can hear speech.

Stratificational

Early reception of Lamb's stratificational grammar (1966) has been guarded. This is understandable, for those who have reviewed it are thoroughly at home in linguistic theory and can adduce a mental glossary of numerous terms for a single part of a language system, can attribute each term correctly to its originator, and can work forward and back from each term to a reconstruction of the theory it comes from. For the student of sign language, however, the interest in stratificational grammar is not its novelty or lack of novelty but its method. Most terms familiar to linguistic theoreticians are appropriate to the parts and relations of a vocal-symbol language. The question that must not be begged at the outset is, which of all the concepts used in linguistic analysis are appropriate to sign language system, and which are not, so that use of the terms for them to name parts of sign language will be metaphor?

It is just here that stratificational analysis shows its worth. Instead of making statements about sign language in terms referring to the parts of another language, the investigator may make use of Lamb's graphing conventions to show relationships. So doing he successfully avoids the problem of giving names to parts and relations before full analysis has been made. To illustrate: the hand with extended index finger, the chin as tab, the sig touch — are these the submorphemic elements of sign language as the writer supposed in 1960, or are they instead the morphemes of the language (Stokoe, 1965)? It may even be that these questions are irrelevant, but a satisfactory answer to any such questions can only follow a reasonably complete account of the whole system; and that is difficult to make unless the questions can be answered at the outset. Lamb's graphs offer a way out of the circle. Instead of naming elements and relations the analyst draws lines between elements with a convention for connections based, like electronic circuit diagrams, on a rigorous logic of relations. Thus the stratificational analyst should be able to amass much information about the system before trying to name either the relation, the system of connections, or the things related, the terminals. He would, however, need to have things to relate. The first or visible stratum of sign language is amenable to modern techniques of direct recording. Paul Ekman (1969) and his associates have described an elaborate computer controlled storage, retrieval, and comparison system they use to study non-verbal behavior, which to the movie or TV camera looks not unlike sign language behavior.

An undetermined number of layers away from this, sign language must have, according to the theory, a stratum which is an interface of language and nonlanguage or meaning. In a sense this too is observable. A sign language request or command translated 'turn off the light' may elicit actions: turning off the light, a blank stare, a smile; or it may elicit other signs: 'what?' 'why?' or 'damn you, do it yourself.' It is possible that drawing the lines, finding the patterns, establishing the intervening strata may be the shortest way to connect the inner structure to the outside worlds of physical and cultural phenomena, and so to describe the language. But it is also possible that the procedure sketched here has a greater chance of success than some others, not because of its theoretical basis, but because using it the researcher may begin with, as his data, everything visible instead of with things assumed to be the elements of sign language.

An example of how stratificational grammar may be adapted to the problems presented by sign language syntax and semology begins with this passage from Lamb: "The sememic sign *mare* connects upward (toward meaning) to a combination of the sememes *female* and *horse*; but the sememic sign *blow up* connects downward (toward speech or writing) to a combination of lexemes *blow* and *up*" (in Hill, 1969: 43). The same procedure allows one to say that the ASL sign 'mother' is a sememic sign that connects upward to sememes *female* and *parent*. *Mother, female,* and *parent* are all sememes, sememic signs, and lexemes in English; but in American Sign Language there is no sememic sign or lexeme 'parents'. Instead the syntactic phrase 'father mother' composed of two signs connects downward to the combination of ASL lexemes 'father' and 'mother'.

Like other descriptive statements the foregoing is subjected to obsolescence by linguistic change. The writer has observed three signers in 1970 using a double tab sign for 'parents'. It has the P-hand as initial dez and makes identical sigs, brushing outward or across, at the temple and jaw tabs. This is cheremically distinguished from 'father' which uses 5-dez and 'mother' which uses the thumb-up A-dez. It seems a coinage likely to survive.

The stratificational terminology and the upward and downward connections in this example serve well to show how easy passage is from sememic and lexemic matters to syntax. In English the sememic sign *parents* is equivalent to the syntactic structure *father and mother* or *mother and father*. But in American Sign Language 'father mother' or 'mother father' is a syntactic combination that connects not upward or downward so much as in a different direction to the two lexemes which are also sememic signs of the language.

It is most important to note that 'father mother' is a completely grammatical combination in this sign language and that it is not an ungrammatical joining of two words as it would be in English.

Once into the stratificational treatment of sign language it is possible to use the same material to look down into the cheremic stratum. American Sign Language, as it may be supposed do all languages, has the sememe *female*; but it has *female* only as a sememe with upward connections to it coming from many sememic signs, also lexemes: the ASL signs for *mother, girl, sister, woman, daughter, lady,* and others. The sememe *female* is only one of the two or more that these connect upward to. Nevertheless the language has no lexeme 'female'. A signer who wants to specify the sex of an animal may use the sign 'girl' even as do some style levels or age grades of English dialects. But translation here is not a sure guide. It would be more in keeping with stratificational theory to state that one sememic sign in English, 'girl', connects upward to sememes *female, young,* and optionally, *human,* but that the sememe *female* does connect downward through several sememic signs and lexemes to these three cheremes: cheek tab, touch sig and downward sig (simultaneously performed).

A more provocative effect of stratificational theory and Lamb's graphic technique is its revelation of the relationship of syntax and semology in American Sign Language. Linear or process grammars, at one stage, postulate surface structures as strings of lexical formatives and grammatical formatives. English seems to have these two kinds of formatives in fairly even proportion, with the latter dividing between affixes and function words. Now American Sign Language has signs which will translate all but a special few (*the, of, a,* and *be*) of the most frequently occurring English function words (see Ch. 4), but it has no grammatical affixes. The one clearcut, i.e. most English-like, derivational affix is the sign often called the 'body sign'. It connects upward with the verb sign used just before it to the sememic sign which in English is written with agentive -*er* suffix. But derivational and inflectional affixes, the formatives so frequently seen and so evenly distributed in English surface structures, seem to be missing from American Sign Language. In all languages which have phonemes as one stratum such affixes are sequential combinations of vowels and consonants with a specialized, non-lexical function. If instead of looking for grammatical formatives that resemble these, one looks at a stratificational model, ASL syntax becomes more understandable.

A further advantage of Lamb's graphic procedure is the attention it focusses on what actually is found in the lower strata. The physical sciences may have developed best by ignoring change — and linguistics would probably not have progressed so far had it not ignored so many of the things that in fact occur along with or as part of verbal behavior. Anthropologists and psychologists, however, sometimes have cause to regret linguists' concentration on the microlinguistic part of the communicative manifold. What is unfortunate or inconvenient for an anthropologist looking at related activities in a culture can be devastating for a linguist looking at a sign language. The separation of paralanguage and kinesics from speech for study, even with the caveat that all three are bound up in one multichannel network, predisposes layman and linguist alike to draw an analogy between what the voice of a speaker does, including paralanguage, and what the hands of a signer do. The unordered, non-sequential connection of sixty or seventy cheremes by threes into sign morphemes cannot give as large a stock as can half as many ordered, sequential, but recurring vocalic and consonantal segments. Along with this disparity in numbers, the presence of grammatical formatives in speech and absence of the same kind of thing among sign lexemes has obscured the true nature of sign language.

Enemies of sign language — and languages as much as religious observances can arouse enmity — argue from the negative characteristics just enumerated that it is a restricted language, poor in vocabulary, and lacking in grammatical-semantic system. As a consequence of such enmity, nowhere in formal educational programs are young deaf children permitted to use what can be their native language for any learning activity (Kohl, 1966; Cicourel and Boese, 1970). As is usual in cases of arbitrarily imposed language policy, the human costs of such misunderstanding of sign language are hard to estimate.

A disinterested scientific view that is comprehensive enough may reveal how a sign language can differ in many ways from all other languages and still be a language "fully developed", as Hoijer puts it, "in every essential aspect" (in Hill, 1969: 51).

Correlational

Appearing at about the same time as Lamb's theory but less well known to American linguists is the correlational theory of Dixon (1965). In some ways the two are antithetical enough to be complementary. Both use for analysis sample texts from tape recorded domestic conversations. Lamb (actually Newell in an appendix, 1966: 71-106) analyzes the relationship between language elements; lexemic system and lexicon, morphemic system and morphicon are shown for the language of the sample. Concentration on connections and the graphic way of working produce four very interesting pictures of NP structure. Dixon begins by correlating situational features, participants in the conversation, and persons talked about, with each other and then moves to the correlations of these with language forms and patterns. Juxtaposition of these two theories with the sample texts analyzed by using each makes clear Dixon's greater emphasis on meaning. He is undismayed by the prospect that several volumes may be needed to detail all the correlations to be found in a text only a few lines long. In contrast Lamb generalizes from a text to a diagrammatic, composite formula for semantic and syntactic phrase-markers that is to be valid for many texts.

Dixon's emphasis on meaning could be salutary in the investigation of sign language. The first question asked by those who newly encounter the language is, "You can't put everything you can say in English into sign language, can you?" The existential answer is "Yes; certainly". But the linguistic question as Dixon might phrase it is, "What meanings can be correlated with sign language patterns?" And after that, "Are these meanings different from those correlated with the patterns of other languages?" Probably the answer to this is yes also. Dixon's theory offers the investigator some useful terminology, if only in "What are the correlations?"

Generative

The theory of language structure called generative or transformational or both names is hardly a single theory. According to one form of it, a generative grammar is a set of rules that operate over an alphabet of symbols representing abstract syntactical categories. The rules generate in a mathematical sense the basic syntactic structures, i.e. strings of symbols, which by a transformational process elsewhere in the grammar acquire both a semantic interpretation and a phonological actualization (Chomsky, 1965). Another form of the theory begins with rules that operate first on a set of distinct semantic features; e.g. a speaker who wants to name the whole class of creatures belonging to the genus Formica has to choose the lexical symbol *ant* with the semantic feature +count, but he must also choose between two constellations of other features presented by the semantic rules. One is —definite, +generic, —aggregate, +plural. The other is —definite, —generic, +aggregate, —plural. These choices respectively give him the nominal *ants* or *the ant*. A third way of beginning a generative grammar uses semantic considerations in a different way. It makes the first rule a rewriting of S as a proposition and a modality with the order unspecified (Fillmore, 1968).

One advantage currently claimed for all varieties of generative linguistic theory is generality or universality. Such universality actually is restrictive, and for all those persons whose native language is sign language, it marks a return to the narrow, mediaeval view of language. That view relegated all who were born deaf or were deafened in infancy to a subhuman status and to inhumane treatment. Before Locke, when speech was generally thought, as it is now by Chomsky and Halle (1968), to be an "*a priori* innate endowment" instead of learned behavior, a deaf-mute was deemed to have neither mind nor soul. The development of a universal theory of language with semantic and phonological parts of the grammar integrated by a syntactic base reverts to outgrown rationalist, and hence restrictive, philosophy.

Proponents of such a theory of linguistics with its central 'transformational cycle' must then suppose that modern deaf persons' sign language is directly derived from some other language, one with a phonological component. Historical fact and easily repeatable observation negate this supposition. Sign language not only presents an obvious exception to phonology-by-rule but it also exhibits a syntax unexplainable by rules in linear sequence. It challenges linguists to seek beyond the accident that most languages are vocal-auditory, to look at the wider field of semiotics, and to ask how human beings order symbols in systems with duality of patterning, for it has a complexity not explained by current model grammars. Instead of positing "an extremely intricate and abstract grammar" (Chomsky and Halle, 1968) that every child acquires to account for the intricate and abstract grammars written to explain that grammar, one who takes the semiotic approach will begin by observing children born deaf in families where only American Sign Language is used or where it is used bilingually with fingerspelled English.

The claim that American Sign Language constitutes an exception to phonology by rule is not hard to substantiate. Current universalist generative theory holds that the intricate, abstract grammar which is every person's heritage ultimately presents surface structures in his own language. These structures are precisely labeled or bracketed strings of formatives. This may be illustrated with the sentence, *The children are watching TV*. (Fig. 5). Before the phonetic rules apply, this was a string of lexical formatives (shown below in italics) and grammatical formatives

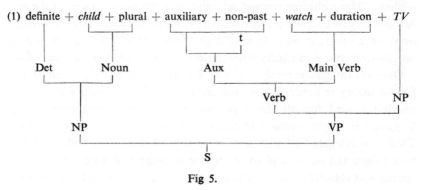

(1) definite + *child* + plural + auxiliary + non-past + *watch* + duration + *TV*

Fig 5.

(shown in Roman Type). Below the string (1) a branching diagram gives the labels and their derivation.

The lexical formatives, says the theory, are syllabic sequences of segments, i.e. vowels and consonants; the grammatical formatives are syllabic or non-syllabic sequences of segments. After certain rules have combined formatives and replaced the separations between them with word boundaries, the string appears like this: (2) ðə + čildrìn + ar + wɔčĭŋ + tiyviy. The most interesting stage of the process follows. By the operation of the transformational cycle, a very few rules are first applied to the material at the outer ends of the branches. Stress patterns (/ᵛ) are assigned to *watching* and *children* before they are assigned to larger structures *(The children; are watching)*. Then structures dominated by nodes closer to S have stress patterns adjusted by the rules. As a result, the syntactic-lexical surface structure (1) is first arranged in a linear sequence of phonetic segments (2), and finally realized with a pattern of stresses assigned by rule in transformational cycling to result in: (3) ðə̀ + číldrìn + ăr + wɔčĭŋ + tíy vìy.

Concomitant with this systematic phonology, as it is called, are the assumptions (a) that vowels and consonants and only they are the essential morphophonemic material and (b) that stress is an automatic result of the syntactic-semantic structure deeper in the grammar than this phonological apparatus.

None of this can apply to sign language for three reasons. First, if vowels and consonants be the two sets of segments in languages universally, then the grammar of any language will specify the relationship of members of the two sets. But the aspects (not segments) of sign language are found in three, not in two sets: tab, dez, and sig (Stokoe, 1960). Nor will an essential two and an automatically adjusted third set, in any combination, fit sign language phenomena.

Second, just as categorical as the statement that two does not equal three, is this: the vocalic and consonantal segments of a language with a phonology must be sequential in time, but the aspects of sign language may and do occur simultaneously. The whole matter of time is immensely complicated in language and linguistics. Stockwell (in Hill, 1969) says of the internal structure of generative grammatical description, that "the sequence is a logical sequence only, though it is spoken of as a sequence of operations which follow each other AS IF in time" [emphasis added]. But even if the sequence of rule operation is logical only, if the phonetic realization emerges from a time-free process, the vowels and consonants human beings speak and hear do follow one another in time. In American

Sign Language however, the kinds of units called 'aspects', meaningless in themselves, that can be substituted for each other to change meaning are kinds that are produced and perceived as separate from one another in space, not in time. The finest divisions or increments of time cannot divide them.

A third reason that systematic phonology is not adaptable to sign language is that it depends completely on the syntactic part of the theory. Consistency is an excellent trait in a grammar describing the interrelation of shape, sense, and sound. The three are so closely related in spoken language that a grammar describing them must be also an almost seamless web. However by the same argument, the shape, sense, and sight of sign language are also interrelated. Then, since the rules for explaining the sound system have no application to the sight system, and since the grammar is all of a piece, the shape (or morphology and syntax) of American Sign Language cannot be described by grammars of this kind,

To answer the question how does sign language syntax differ from other or 'universal' syntax? would be easier if one knew more, absolutely, about it. Written and spoken languages have been the object of grammatical study for five thousand years or more, but while sign languages have often aroused interest, they are so different as to have escaped much linguistic scrutiny. As recently as 1960 writers who can be credited with some knowledge of sign language were claiming that it had no grammar or syntax.

Some linguists, on the other hand, have supposed that once the sight system of a sign language had been described, even if by the despised autononomous or taxonomic methods, there would emerge formatives, i.e. morphemes and lexemes, strings of which could be traced back through transformations to deep structures (of universal syntax) whence they had come.

Would that such theorists were correct. In that case the learning of a second language would be far easier and would be done more often and more successfully than in fact it is by deaf persons fluent in sign language. Instead the sight, shape, and sense systems of sign language seem to be just similar enough, yet enough different, to cause maximum difficulty, maximum negative interference for the person learning English as a second language.

Although the general theory seems incompatible with the system of sign language as that is becoming clearer, the use of generative techniques can be very helpful, especially in contrastive study of American

Sign Language and English. As a hypothesis recognized as empirically indeterminate, even the notion of a universal deep structure may make sign language syntax easier to explain to English speakers. To illustrate, let us say that a sentence of a certain type in all languages consists of proposition and modality. Proposition can then be rewritten as NP and VP, and one possible choice of modality is assertion. Here is enough to begin with. The type of sentence this describes says something (M) about a person (NP) and what he is feeling (VP). So far English and sign language can be said to share this structure. But to get an actual sentence the modality requires, in English, that VP develop a branching structure that eventually ends in a non-past, third-person singular form of the copula, *is,* and an adjective, *angry.* The full sentence may be, *He is angry.* In American Sign Language the modality requires that VP precede NP and that the signer's direction of glance and facial expression add other kinds of meaning to the two-sign sentence: 'angry' 'he'. It is most important to note that this kind of procedure necessitates careful distinction and separation from other kinds of description. While the sign language novice may be encouraged to find that American Sign Language and English sentences that say the same thing have the same deep structure, he is likely to be put off by finding 'angry' called a verb. Of course the proper use of this procedure does no such thing. Not everything in an NP branch is a noun nor everything in a VP branch a verb. Some treatments of this kind make the contrast easier to take by withholding the name of verb from the copula. The absence of the copula from sign language is a fact to be learned along with the information that the same ASL sign in some sentences would best be translated 'angry', in others 'anger', and in still others 'getting angry' or 'get angry'.

In this connection it is possible to review briefly the "Generative Grammar of Sign" by McCall (1965). As a first attempt to describe sign language syntax it is commendable, but the strong tradition of sign-for-word translation keeps it from being in fact a grammar of American Sign Language. Taking a number of sign conversations recorded at a social gathering, she first had the sign strings translated into English word strings; and the part of speech labels unfortunately cling too strongly to the words for the symbols in her rules to be other than English grammatical categories. Sign language, like Chinese, is a system in which the same lexical form in one place may be adjective, in another noun, and in a third, verb. Again the situation calls for care in the use of generative theory and technique. Hypothesizing the deep structure and examining the English and sign occurrences against it should be a way to keep categories clear and error at a minimum. A great virtue of McCall's thesis is that it shows how complete a grammar there is in sign language and how little need to apologize for inadequacies of the system itself. Indeed the use of one or another theory of grammar is far less productive of error in describing sign language than a positive bias conscious or unconscious against its use and against any attempt to treat it linguistically. Another source of error from which McCall's grammar is largely free comes from the use of at least two varieties of American Sign Language for different functions (Ch. 8). Because her corpus was gathered in an informal situation, McCall has a preponderance of sentences which in fact have ASL syntax and do not follow the order of sentences generated in English and translated. But diglossia in sign language is not easily handled by strictly linear generative grammars; and humor, metaphor, and various style levels which change the determination of what is grammatical and what is not also make the use of the generative model difficult.

Operational

The last of the seven theoretical models for use in sign language linguistics to be reviewed here is not as well known as the others. It has its origin in the philosophy of operationalism (Ceccato, 1961) and breaks with most linguistic tradition as these statements indicate: "Operations are the content of thought; thought is the content of language". One operation, correlation, assigns a particular temporal order to three things. The first is present to the attention at the time of its production and then is maintained in attention while a second thing is presented. This in turn is maintained in attention along with the first while a third thing is presented. At that time the correlation is made or 'closed'. Fig. 6 shows the operation of correlation diagrammatically. A correla-

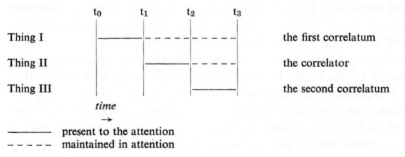

Fig. 6.

tion read from left to right presents a fixed order of thought, but the
linear order of input words may be different; moreover a correlation
may be presented as a correlatum in another correlation. In Fig. 7 the
whole of correlation A is the first correlatum in B as C is the first correlatum of D, and D is the second correlatum of B. This graphical representation of correlations is cumbersome, though it shows the operation
clearly; so Ceccato and his associates use a rectangular graph, derived
as shown in Fig. 8. Using this convention, a correlation net, the same
one shown in Fig. 7, looks like Fig. 9 when the lines connecting rectangles
are added. Further explanation of the operation of correlating will
accompany the examples to be presented. The sentence below, produced
in writing by a college student, a technical bilingual, as the body of
a note written to a dormitory supervisor, was at first a complete puzzle
as an English sentence: (i) *I will instead you for my surprise*. The technical
bilingual (Lambert, 1963) in this case is a native signer of American
Sign Language who generates sentences in that language and translates
them into English which he has been taught in school but which he
knows better as a word-for-sign glossary than as a syntactic-semantic
system. When (i) was read by its recipient as a sign sentence, the words
standing one by one for signs in that order, it had only to be signed
overtly to become perfectly clear, although not easily translatable into
English.

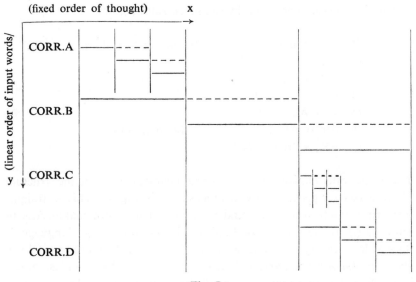

Fig. 7.

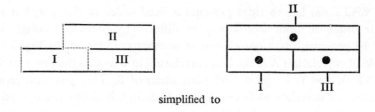

simplified to

Fig. 8.

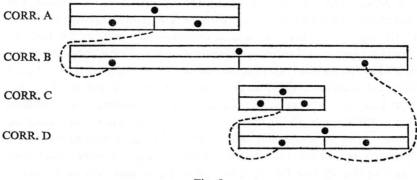

Fig. 9.

Even without translation it is near enough to English to be assigned to a basic structure generated by the seven rules below:

(1) S → Nuc (+ Per)   'nucleus'; 'peripheral material'
(2) Nuc → NP + VP
(3) NP → Pro, Det + N
(4) VP → V + NP
(5) V → Aux + Verb
(6) Per → AP ...   'adverbial phrase'
(7) AP → Prep + NP

These rules offer choices, but when certain choices are made the structure of sentence (i) is generated by them as shown in Fig. 10. This is straightforward syntactical analysis, and while it still does not make sense of sentence (i) to the speaker of English who knows no sign language, it does at least certify that sentence (i) is identical in structure to (ii) *I will want you for my foursome.* It is a structure shared by countless others in English. The two sentences are identical in structure, that is to say,

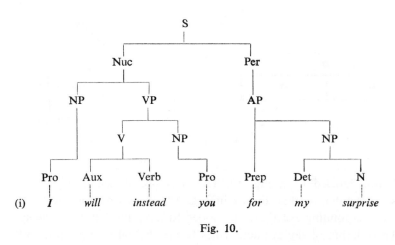

Fig. 10.

if the sign glossed 'instead' can be a verb in American Sign Language. As a matter of fact, the sign is sometimes glossed 'replace' or 'exchange' when it is used as a verb; but using them for *instead* still produces sentences that look incongruous or ungrammatical to the reader of English: (iii) ? *I will replace you for my surprise*; (iv) *I will exchange you for my surprise*. Another gloss 'substitute' gets no closer to a sensible English sentence. Nevertheless the structure, as syntax, is the same for the sign sentence (i) as for the proper English sentence (ii). The question is whether English has in its lexicon a single verb to gloss the verb sign in (i) which will both translate the sentence and preserve the structure.

While the question of translation is still open, let us see how sentence (i) would be treated in the correlational analysis of operational linguistics.

The first analytical operation is to enter the first word, i.e. the first sign, of the sentence in an open correlation rectangle. All three places are open, but 'I' as the first sign is most likely to be the first thing to be correlated and may tentatively be entered in the lower left cell. The two signs 'I' and 'will' make a correlation when the second is final, but in sentence (i) there are other signs and other correlations to be considered. The signs 'will' and 'instead' are correlata of one of these; its correlator is the operation that joins them into a language element, an idiom, when one follows the other in the order given. Fig. 11 shows both this correlation and the equivalent portion of the generative P-marker. This correlation now can be used as the second correlatum of the correlation into which 'I' was put as first. But note that the same correlation of 'will' and 'instead' is also the first correlatum of a third

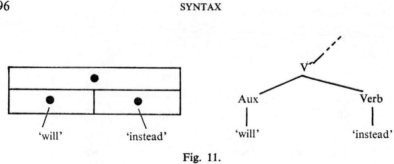

Fig. 11.

correlation, labeled C in Fig. 12. The structure shown in Fig. 12 is somewhat similar to that shown in Fig. 10; the correlators in A, B, and C corresponding exactly to the nodes Nuc, V, and VP, respectively. But the ordering of the syntactic rules forces the rules to generate VP after Nuc and V after VP, while the correlational net follows the "linear order of input words" (Maretti in Ceccato, 1961: 149) downward and the "fixed order of thought" *(ibid.)* from left to right. The semi-lattice (the mathematical form of a generative P-marker) shown in Fig. 10 plots linear but time-free branching. The correlational net in Fig. 12 plots thought, i.e. operations in time, against time order of words.

Another difference between generative theory and operational theory is seen as soon as the last three signs of sentence (i) are entered in correlation graphs. The sign 'for', like English *for* and Italian *por,* is a correlator instead of a correlatum. It has to be entered in the upper cell of a rectangle graph and will not do in either of the correlatum spots. What 'for' correlates in sentence (i) is the whole net of Fig. 12 with the

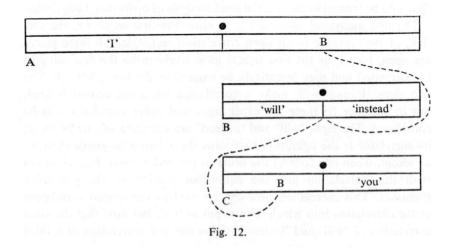

Fig. 12.

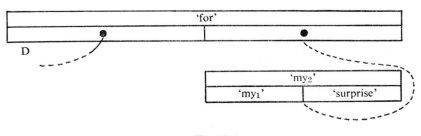

Fig. 13.

correlation which follows (Fig. 13). The next sign of sentence (i) translated 'my' serves two functions, fills two cells of a rectangle, is both
correlator and first correlatum. The last three signs of sentence (i) form
the correlational net shown in Fig. 13. The contents of the upper cells
of the rectangles in Fig. 13, the correlators, do not match nodes in the
right branch of the P-marker of Fig. 10. Instead the correlators are signs
and therefore they might be called part of the surface of sign language,
if one were to use the terminology of the generative theory, and not
part of the (deep) structure at all. But when the operation of correlation
is considered, there can be no doubt that 'for' serves very well the
function of connecting two language constructions in a meaningful way.
In Fig. 14 the whole net of sentence (i) correlations is set opposite the
complete P-marker. The two graphic analyses of the sentence in this
figure show both similarity and difference. One important difference is
that operational analysis attributes various roles to morphemes or signs,
whereas phrase-structure analysis attributes only surface or linear functions to them; e.g. the sign glossed 'my' serves both as first correlatum
indicating the signer and as correlator symbolizing possession, the
relation between signer and 'surprise'; but according to the other theory
'my' is simply a determiner because NP has Det + N. This difference
is crucial. Operational analysis purports to find the operations of thought
denoted by the correlations of the language units actually used, i.e. the
sign morphemes. The phrase-structure grammar first generates twelve
abstract syntactical entities which can then be replaced by the morphemes, i.e. Nuc, NP, Pro, VP, V, A, Verb, Per, AP, Prep, Det, N.
   Another important difference is the explicit disagreement of the two
analyses as to order. The P-marker in Fig. 14 and all other generative
grammars the writer can recall agree that V or the symbol which may
be rewritten as Aux + Verb cannot appear before VP, because V is
generated from VP (rule 4 above). But the correlation (B) of 'will' with

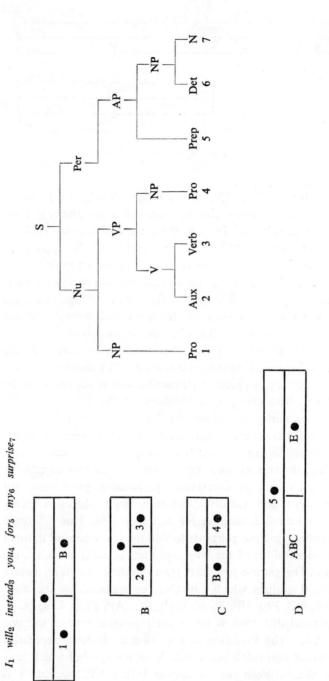

Fig. 14.

'instead' takes place before the correlation of B with 'you'. The order of signs in time is represented by the order of the rectangles from top to bottom. The order of correlating operations is shown by the left to right dimension. If correlation B is taken as equivalent to 'rewrite V as Aux plus Verb', then it clearly closes before correlation C closes, but correlation C is equivalent to 'rewrite VP as V plus NP'. Any resolution of this problem of order must be sought in a larger field than that afforded by American Sign Language syntax. In the interim the different results to be obtained by using these two methods of parsing sentences can be used to gain perspective on the structure of that language.

A promising approach to contrastive linguistic analysis begins with the hypothesis that sentences produced in two languages to translate each other share the same structure. One then looks to different transformations of that structure into actual sentences for the explanation of their difference. Using this approach one assumes that these sentences have the same syntactic-semantic structure: (v) *He left yesterday*; and (vi) 'he' 'yesterday' 'leave'. A simple grammar will suffice to generate the hypothetical structure: (1) S → Nuc + Per; (2) Nuc → NP + VP; (3) Per → Adv. The lexicons for the two languages so far are also simple and nearly symmetrical, i.e. NP: /hiy/ 'he'; VP /left/ 'leave'; Adv: /yestirdiy/ 'yesterday'. All that remains is a statement to the effect that in the American Sign Language grammar a transformation transposes the order of VP and Adv. It may not be pertinent to enquire why the order generated by the rules is primordial. A linguist whose native language was American Sign Language might have begun with a grammar of two rules: (1) S → NP + VP; (2) VP → Anteverb + Verb. Then the lexicon for both languages would have no heading Adv but would have after Anteverb: /yestirdiy/ 'yesterday'. Next, in order to explain the difference, the grammar of English would need a transformation causing the verb and anteverb to change places. A more complete grammar would also show that on occasion it is Anteverb and NP that change, yielding the grammatical sentence, Yesterday he left.

Of course all this is speculation. There is as yet no generative grammar of American Sign Language written by a native signer. To return to the three-rule grammar for the structure that the two sentences hypothetically share, the addition of another rule makes a more explicit generation of the English sentence (rule (2a) VP → tense + Verb). This entails some change in the lexicon or morphophonemic rules for proceeding from the string, NP + t + V + Adv, to the surface, *He left yesterday*.

But all this requires a major change in the grammar of the sign language sentence. The second branch of the first rule is not relevant. The two grammars as now emended are shown in Fig. 15 with the new arrangement of the lexicon for each below the rules. For some uses this contrastive analysis will suffice, but for use by teachers whose training in grammar has followed traditional lines it will be less than satisfactory to find that 'yesterday' in sign language is a verb tense instead of an adverb of time and that in sign language verb tense is manifested by a free sign morpheme placed before the verb. Unfortunately these teachers may already have been made uncomfortable by learning that modern grammarians insist that the tense must be generated before the verb in all languages.

	English			ASL
	(1) S → Nucleus + Periphery			(1) S → Nucleus
	(2) Nu → NP + VP			(2) Nu → NP + VP
	(2a) VP → t + V			(2a) VP → t + V
	(3) Pe → Adv			

	NP	tense	Verb	Adverb
ASL	'he'	'yesterday'	'leave'	————
Eng	/hiy/	/-d/ : /-iyv/ /-eft/	/liyv/	/yestirdiy/

Fig. 15.

An alternative to doing contrastive analysis on this model is to take the sentences of the two languages as correlations or nets of correlations. The diagrams in Fig. 16 (after Ceccato, 1961) differ. The implication in them is that the structures differ as well. From left to right the diagrams present the order in which the operations of correlating occur. From top to bottom they present the order of words or signs in the sentences given. In the English sentence, the word *he* is first present to

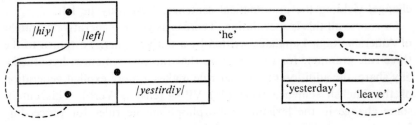

Fig. 16.

49849

the attention through hearing, but after it is spoken and heard it is still maintained in attention while the word *left* is heard. Then both are maintained in attention until *yesterday* is heard. The first correlation closes with the end of the presence of *left,* but the second correlation uses the first as its first correlatum and hence cannot close until *yesterday* is presented.

The graphs show the difference more immediately than can a description of the operations. Nevertheless, in the ASL sentence, the first correlation remains open until the second is closed and presented as its second correlatum. What it means to close or complete a correlation may be explained in semological terms, in syntactical terms, or in phonological terms, or in all three; although Ceccato, the originator of the theory with its diagrams of correlations, would eschew all three. At least this much is clear: in the English sentence the structure made by the first two words is then connected to the third. In the ASL sentence the first sign is maintained in attention (held in short-term storage some psycholinguists would say) until the structure made by the second and third sign can be connected to it. As another way, besides the graphical means used in Fig. 16 and the rhetorical used just above to state the difference in the sentences, an algebraic expression may be used. If parentheses are used in their usual algebraic sense and if 'o' represents the operation of correlating, then the English sentence is expressible as: *(He ° left) ° yesterday.* The sign language sentence has this form: 'He' ° ('yesterday' ° 'leave'). Note that the last sign could if one wished be glossed 'left', but just as Hungarian can express plural by placing the unpluralized noun after a numeral adjective, so sign language can express past by placing the uninflected verb sign after a sign denoting past time. At any rate, a great deal more than is now known about the nature of syntactic operations will have to be discovered before one could say with assurance that the English sentence and the ASL sentence have the same structure.

An even clearer instance of structural difference between sentences that translate each other is given by the two pairs of sentences analyzed in Fig. 17. Expressing the same relations algebraically becomes complicated because *is,* the form of the copula in the English examples, already symbolizes connection: in the terminology of operational linguistics, it is a correlator. Besides algebra can either represent word/ sign order or show the time order of correlation, but it cannot do both at once. Therefore if 'x' represents *he* and 'y' represents *sick,* the first sentence is simply (x is y). Likewise with 'm' for Doctor and 'n' for

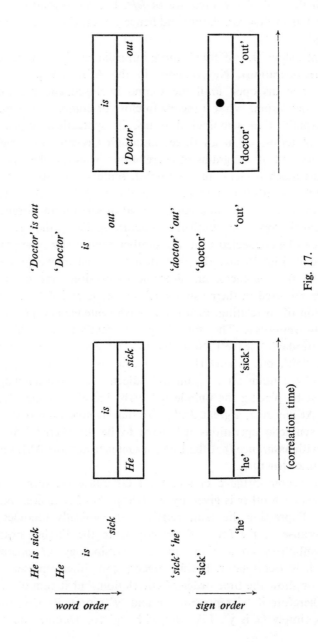

Fig. 17.

out, the second sentence is (m is n). In the sentences of American Sign Language an overt symbol must be used for the operation of joining x and y; so let 'o' be correlator. Then the order of the signs in the first ASL sentence is (y o x), but the order of the correlation is (x o y). The remaining sentence in both orders has the structure (m o n), but ASL informants accept reversed sign order (n o m) as equally grammatical.

If very similar sentences in English and in American Sign Language can occasion such different analyses as the sentences in Fig. 17 have called for, analyzing a pair of sentences that seem to be very different reveals an unsuspected identity in structure but considerable difference in the semiotic systems of the two languages. The English sentence, *I have something in reserve* almost exactly translates this two-sign sentence of American Sign Language: 'have' 'behind'. The five-word English sentence makes a net of only three correlations, because one of its words is a correlator. The two-sign sentence, however, also makes a net of three correlations as Fig. 18 shows. The correlational structure of these sentences is identical, as will be seen if the words on the left and the signs on the right are removed, leaving only the rectangles and the lines joining them. What makes the sentences different is the different way words and signs used in them function. *In,* the English word which serves as correlator needs no further explanation, but the semiotic features of the ASL signs need to be explored.

The sign glossed 'have' brings the dez, usually both hands, in B configuration inward to touch (sig) the chest (tab). There may be some

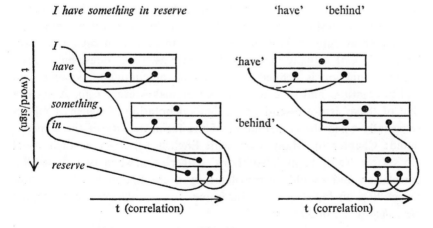

Fig. 18.

similarity between this sign as a gesture and the concept of possession; if so the sign 'have' has iconic qualities. However as a morpheme of American Sign Language it also functions symbolically because by convention it denotes not the abstraction 'possession' but the whole intensional class of having; i.e. it translates the transitive verbs *have, avoir, haben* in most of their senses. In the example of Fig. 18 moreover, it adds still another function to its symbolic and perhaps iconic relation to its denotatum. It also points to the signer and so it functions as index as well. This is the reason it is shown in Fig. 18 as present in three cells. The parenthetical (I) there is in fact indicated both by the sig of 'have' and by what the signer's face does.

The sign 'behind', however, in this sign sentence adds to its usual iconic function a second iconic function. The tab hand is A. The dez, also A, moves around behind tab and touches the wrist, or is checked in a definite tandem position. Since the sig puts dez A behind tab A, the sign's action is iconic; similarity between the sign and the relation designated *behind* in English is so obvious that some observers are misled into thinking that all sign language is like this. But the dez of 'behind' is also visible and it is difficult to say whether it shows similarity (iconicity) to 'something', or whether it is 'something' (symbolism). However the relation of sign to its denotata, the important point illustrated by the ASL sentence in Fig. 18, must be that 'behind' as a sign denotes both the second correlatum and the first as well in a correlation which in English is filled by three words, *something in reserve*.

The two special features of the signs in this sentence are not rare in American Sign Language (nor in language as the bad Latin *habeo reservatum* might suggest). In fact, unless there is an explicit denotation of a different subject, a verb sign denotes both its lexical meaning and the signer as subject. Not all verb signs in American Sign Language have a sig that actually indicates the signer as 'have' does; but indexic semiotic function is defined as some kind of contiguity between sign and denotatum, and of course the signer makes every sign. A sig like that of 'have' is not essential to a sign's denotation of signer as subject (especially when the contribution of the facial activity of the signer is noted: Chapter 6). Many signs with English adjectives as their usual glosses, e.g. 'sad', 'happy', 'stubborn', 'eager', etc., when used alone fill a correlation and should be translated by a correlation not by a word. Depending on facial activity the frames for translation are: *I am ...*; *He (she) is ...*; or *Are you ...*?

Pursuing this kind of contrastive study might reveal that the signs of

American Sign Language are semiotically less differentiated than are the words or morphemes of English. Having a tab, a sign not normally indexic can on occasion denote a substantive, e.g. as 'have' denotes 'I have' unless another subject is signed or facially indicated. Having a dez, a sign not usually iconic may represent an object, concrete or symbolic, in addition to its usual denotatum, e.g. 'something in reserve'. And having a sig, a sign used to denote relationship may also imitate action iconically, e.g. the sign that usually translates out may mean 'go out' or 'resign', as the sign 'in' may mean 'put in', 'stuff', 'insert'.

These potentialities of the ASL sign to be used with different semiotic, hence syntactic and semantic, functions should not be taken as they already have been inchoately by enemies of sign language to prove primitivism. Much more in keeping with empirical data is the conclusion that a language whose distinctive features are visible in three dimensional space, in time, and in ineluctable connection with at least one user of that language of necessity has different morphology, syntax, grammar, lexicon, semantics, semology, and redundancy from those of a spoken (and written) language. All unbiased anthropological linguistic studies have shown that a language with a complex system of vowel harmony works no better nor worse than one without it, that a language with almost every form class heavily inflected is neither superior nor inferior to an uninflected language, that a people with many terms for objects somehow related but no term for the class are no more nor less human than a people with a word for the class but no specific names for its members. It would not even be justifiable to conclude that users of sign language always make effective and economical use of the undifferentiated semiotic functions potentially combined in its signs. Some of them do, but this is a special not a general truth. Some users of English also make effective and economical use of its differentiated semiotic functions, i.e. its rich vocabulary. Obviously this kind of statement is not a characterization of a language as a semiotic system but an observation about particular persons and particular language use. The important concomitant of the variable semiotic functions of signs is that sign sentences do not look like English sentences. The structures of sign sentences sometimes resemble and sometimes differ from the structures of English sentences. But even sentences that are translations of each other in English and in American Sign Language may have either identical or radically different structure. And if the syntax of the two languages presents a complex contrast, their semantic systems including the two lexicons are even further from being congruent systems.

Difference in syntax determines lexical-semantic difference; but it is often assumed, tacitly and otherwise, that because the two languages occur in the same geographical regions, in the same cultural setting, and even in the bilingual competence of the same individual there must be a uniform relation between word, sign, and meaning. English-to-sign manuals are compiled on this assumption, but no such relation exists.

Meaning in American Sign Language is to a surprisingly large extent conveyed by visual phenomena not contained in signs, i.e. if signs are defined as is usual in handbooks giving signs as equivalents for words. Lexical signs, and function signs for making phrases and sentences, the language has in sufficient number (Chapter 4); but a number of semiotic signs that any language needs to make its system complete will seem to be lacking from American Sign Language if the only kind of sign described is a form of manual activity. These non-manual semiotic signs will be considered in the following chapter.

REFERENCES, CHAPTER 5

Bloomfield, Leonard,
    1926   "A Set of Postulates for the Science of Language", *Lg.* 2, 153-164.
Ceccato, Silvio,
    1961   *Linguistic Analysis and Programming for Mechanical Translation* (New York, Gordon and Breach).
Chomsky, Noam,
    1965   *Aspects of the Theory of Syntax* (Cambridge, Mass., M.I.T. Press).
Chomsky, Noam, and Morris Halle,
    1968   *The Sound Pattern of English* (New York, Harper and Row).
Cicourel, Aaron V., and B. Boese,
    1971   "Sign Language Acquisition and the Teaching of Deaf Children", *The Functions of Language,* ed. by Dell Hymes *et al.* (New York, Teachers College Press).
Dixon, Robert M. W.,
    1965   *What is Language ? A New Approach to Linguistic Description* (London, Longmans).
Ekman, Paul, and Wallace V. Friesen,
    1969   "The Repertoire of Nonverbal Behavior — Categories, Origins, Usage, and Coding", *Semiotica,* 1:1, 49-98.
Fillmore, Charles,
    1968   "The Case for Case", *Universals in Linguistic Theory,* ed. by Bach and Harms (New York, Holt).
Gleason, Henry A., Jr.,
    1965   *Linguistics and English Grammar* (New York, Holt).
Hill, Archibald A. (ed.),
    1969   *Linguistics Today* (New York, Basic Books).
Hoijer, Harry,
    1969   "The Origin of Language", *Linguistics Today,* ed. by Hill (New York, Basic Books), 50-58.

Kohl, Herbert R.,
1966 *Language and Education of Deaf Children* (New York, Center for Urban Education).

Lamb, Sydney M.,
1966 *Outline of Stratificational Grammar* (Washington, D.C., Georgetown University Press).
1969 "Lexicology and Semantics", *Linguistics Today,* ed. by A. A. Hill (New York, Basic Books), 40-49.

Lambert, Wallace,
1963 "On Second Language Learning and Bilingualism", *Teaching English as a Second Language,* ed. by H. B. Allen (New York, McGraw-Hill).

Lewis, M. M.,
1968 *The Education of Deaf Children* (London, H.M.S.O.).

McCall, Elizabeth A.,
1965 "A Generative Grammar of Sign", M.A. thesis (University of Iowa).

Mallery, Garrick,
1881 "Sign Language among North American Indians", *First Annual Report of the Bureau of American Ethnology,* ed. by J. W. Powell, 263-552.

Pesonen, Jaako,
1968 *Phoneme Communication of the Deaf* (= *AASF,* ser. B, 151, 2).

Pike, Kenneth,
1954, 1955, 1960 *Language in Relation to a Unified Theory of the Structure of Human Behavior* (Glendale, Cal., Summer Institute of Linguistics).

Program of Washington Linguistics Club,
1967 (March).

Stockwell, Robert,
1969 "Generative Grammar", *Linguistics Today,* ed. by A. A. Hill (New York, Basic Books), 259-269.

Stokoe, William C., Jr.,
1960 "Sign Language Structure: An Outline of the Visual Communication Systems of the American Deaf", *SIL:* O.P. 8 (Reissued Washington, D.C., Gallaudet College Press).

Stokoe, William C., Jr., C. Croneberg and D. Casterline,
1965 *A Dictionary of American Sign Language* (Washington, D.C., Gallaudet College Press).

Trager, George L.,
1963 "Linguistics is Linguistics", *SIL:* O.P. 10.

West, LaMont, Jr.,
1960 "The Sign Language: An Analysis", Unpublished Ph. D. Dissertation (Indiana University).

6

SEMOLOGY

A sentence of American Sign Language when looked at as composed of manual activity, signs, and of significant structures, syntax, is incomplete; for it is also a message or a meaning. In fact, the meaning or message is its real reason for being. However, little of significance about sign language semology can be stated at this point by statements based entirely on what has so far been described. What is required is an approach to the whole semiotic system as if, for the moment, all that has been said and written about manual gestures and sign language did not exist. Seen thus the system is visual, not auditory, tactile, nor chemical; the material of its sign vehicle is somatic activity. What the addressee receives though is not a view of the signer's hands alone but an entire view of the whole person signing. And what is signified by this sight is like what is signified by any language act.

If it were possible to include within these pages two short films of two sign languages being used, all this would be much clearer. Unfortunately technology lags. One film the writer and others have seen, made by the University of Oklahoma Department of Sociology, describes briefly the Indian Sign Language. At first a voice on the sound track translates a sign vocally in English as an actor on camera demonstrates repeatedly. When sufficient manual vocabulary has thus been introduced, the film shows a narrative performance, complete with an audience, or addressees, who occasionally comment or ask questions and receive replies, all in signs. A most notable feature of this film to one who knows American Sign Language is the facial activity of the Indian actor-narrator. Its expression of dignified solemnity never changes, although the actor's eyes do follow his hands sometimes and lower with the hands at the clause endings.

If a conversation could be filmed of American Sign Language in use among three or four native signers of comparable age and social status to the Indians in this film, the most striking difference would be that in facial expression and activity. Deaf signer's faces are not impassive but would be judged by observers from general American culture to be exceptionally expressive; i.e. signers share a general American kinesic system. However, in addition to denoting the kinds of things usual in American kinesics, facial and bodily actions are also part of the linguistic system of American Sign Language and have an importance unsuspected by the observer who is not a user of the language.

Viewed semologically, then, as visible activity plus syntactic structure plus meaning, a sentence, S, of American Sign Language may be seen to have two sensible components which are both vehicles for its intelligible import. In a radical modification of a familiar convention, S → F/M: a sentence of American Sign Language has two components, F, the facial, and M, the manual. Both are present at once; neither can be said to precede the other. It is physiologically normal, however, for the signer's face to appear most of the time above the signer's hands, so that the convention observed in writing the expression, S → F/M, uses the virgule to show this spatial not temporal relationship. The expression is then read, 'A sentence of American Sign Language has a facial component appearing over, but at the same time with, a manual component'.

The first semological rule of ASL structure may or may not be true of Indian Sign Language. Nothing in the literature contradicts the impression made by the Oklahoma film that an impassivity of countenance is part of the ISL system. Moreover, its uses, now for formal storytelling and the preservation of folk tradition, formerly for treaty making and important exchanges in military or hunting expeditions, suggest that the dignified, unmoving face of the signer is part of the system.

A more important psycholinguistic, sociolinguistic, and physiolinguistic contrast may also be seen in this difference between ASL facial activity and ISL impassivity. The native signers of the former language are deaf. For them a sentence, S, a semological unit, is a unit of American Sign Language. All that can be put into such a unit of language is in it; and since it is in their native language, the sum of possible sentences in it comes very close to summing up them and their culture. On the other hand, the early users of Indian Sign Language were persons who could hear and therefore who had as native language one or another tongue with its own full phonological, morphological, and semological systems. To them then a sentence in Indian Sign Language was a (perhaps unusually ordered) sentence of their native language encoded by a formal, conventional code in which lexical units as gross grammatical units; e.g. uninflected nouns and verbs were represented by manual signs. There would have been no advantage if these ISL users had spoken aloud or utilized the facial gestures (if any) of their culture's kinesics. To the addressee engaged in decoding ISL sentences into a different language, his own, any such facial additions to what he saw would be outside the conventions of the code and would surely interfere with his task.

What makes this basic difference between ASL semology and ISL semology difficult to discern and so long in coming to light is that deaf persons sometimes, and the majority of hearing persons who communicate with them regularly, in fact use signs in a way completely analogous to Indian Sign Language; i.e. they encode English sentences by a formal, conventional code in which lexical and gross grammatical units of English are represented by manual signs. There is one difference: persons using this code, called Signed English (Stokoe, 1970) have or act as if they had English as a native language. They may therefore speak the words while performing the signs (the Simultaneous Method) or go through the motions of speaking without uttering sound.

Following this contrast of two distinct semiotic modes, of linguistic versus substitution-code signing, it is well to reiterate the first semological rule of American Sign Language: a sentence has a facial component appearing over and at the same time with a manual component. This rule does not divide anything into immediate constituents but specifies a juxtaposition of components. There is nothing in the rule to preclude the facial component from carrying one message and the manual another, or even to prohibit a conflict in the import of the two. In fact this happens: a signer's hand may be performing the sign 'like' while his face and head are signalling negation. The whole sentence would be translated, 'I don't like it' or 'I didn't like it'.

To some extent this separation of messages occurs in other than ASL cultures. Those familiar wirh the work of Trager, Smith, Hall, and Birdwhistell will recall their characterization of human communicative activity as a multichannel manifold. The convention of the virgule in the first semological rule may be extended to cover figurative superposition (and possibly semiotic evolution); then one may represent the totality of a communication, C, as proxemics/kinesics/paralanguage/ language. At least four messages may be in simultaneous process accord-

ing to this scheme. Whether they harmonize or conflict is partly determined by the speaker's choice; otherwise it is determined by his culture,
i.e. by what interpretation members of the culture put on the signs of
the first three component semiotic systems.

It is tempting to see a parallel between this four-channel complex of
normal spoken communication and the facial/manual composition of
American Sign Language. Proxemics and kinesics are largely visual
systems, while paralanguage and speech are audible. If the communication manifold, C, of normal spoken interaction is then represented as
made up of visible, Vi, and audible, Au, components, the parallel to
S → F/M seems very close. The next step is to show proxemics and
kinesics as simultaneous components of the visible communicative mode,
or Vi → Pr/Ki. Likewise the audible is made up of superposed paralanguage and speech, or Au → Pa/Sp. This can all be shown in a semi-
lattice, Fig. 19. There is no need for the virgules when a two-dimensional
representation is used.

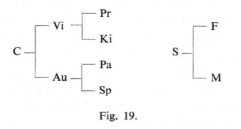

Fig. 19.

However a closer examination shows that normal spoken communication is not at all parallel to the structure of American Sign Language.
Although there are many parallels, some of them drawn in the earlier
chapters, between the manual component, M, of sign language and the
morphemic or verbal units of spoken language, Sp, and although many
resemblances can be seen, particularly in the sign vehicles themselves,
between the facial component, F, and the visible component, Vi, the
difference of the two systems is inescapable. Spoken language, Sp in
Fig. 19, is of course the initial S of all generative grammars; but again
in Fig. 19, Sp is not equal to S, the sentence of American Sign Language,
nor is the American Sign Language sentence system congruent with the
S of other languages. In an ASL sentence two kinds of visible semiotic
systems are components of S, and S is not a component of anything else.

The obvious difference between sign language and other languages is
this difference in primary sensory modality, but the major linguistic or

semiotic difference is that sign language is itself dual-channel activity. In other languages there is a very thorough specialization of the fourth channel, Sp, leaving the other three a different sort of message to handle. While proxemics, kinesics, and paralanguage all convey messages and constitute very interesting semiotic systems; none of them has the dual patterning of language. They have elements and meanings. They can be analyzed as unit, profile, system or set, isolate, pattern; but they do not have adjustable syntax and do not operate for long independently of language. The messages they carry can all be more or less easily expressed in language, but there are things said in language which they cannot express. The case is otherwise with the two components of American Sign Language. To a limited extent the facial and the manual components can work independently and may substitute for each other. 'Yes' and 'no', for instance, can be exclusively facial or exclusively manual. But this is extrasyntactical. The syntax of sign language sentences requires the presence of both components.

Segmental and supersegmental phonemes may make a closer analogue to the manual and facial components of American Sign Language than do speech and its paralinguistic and visible accompaniments. Like the former pair the components of sign language are simultaneously present to the attention. Pitch, stress, and juncture phenomena are not super-posed to vowels and consonants in any spatial sense, but they are produced simultaneously with them, and they do carry a different message or make different kinds of signals. However the analogy is still not close. Stress, pitch, and juncture as one component and vowels and consonants as another are abstractions from the whole flow of speech sound. Their separation is needed for analytical purposes, which of course is why they are spoken of separately and given separate terms, but producing one or two without the others is hardly possible; e.g. there is just no producing /instæntliy/ without stress or pitch any more than of saying /ˈ˄ ˘/. But facial and manual components of American Sign Language do have separate reality. T. H. Gallaudet writes of his ability to produce a complete short narrative in sign language without any use of his hands at all (1847). And deaf students have some interest-ing variations on the old parlor game in which players try to select their partners when hands or feet alone are visible. One version puts the signer behind a curtain or board with armholes and a painted human facade. The fun comes in trying to guess what is being signed by the person whose arms project through the holes. It is difficult because the facial component is missing. Another version introduces even more possibility of error, hence more amusement. Two players stand in close tandem, the one in the rear reaching around supplies the manual part, the one in front the facial.

The use of the face for signalling the differences between assertion, negation, and question has been noted before (Stokoe, 1960: 63-65; 1965: 275). And notice has also been made of the fact that 'I' rarely needs signing because the signer's self is part of the denotatum of a verb sign, because of the iconic or indexic nature of the sign, and because 'I' is understood as subject unless another person is indicated after the verb sign. But a native user of the language does not need to wait to know whether the signer or another person will be indicated as subject; the facial component makes that clear even as the verb sign is being performed.

It is the combination of these two kinds of function that make the dual-channel sign language composition unique. If the facial component were used only to signal question, negation, assertion, command, and the like, it might be considered a close analogue of intonation features. If it were used only to mean 'I', 'you', 'he', 'back there', and such things, which uses it does have, then it should be analyzable into morphemes which could be listed in the lexicon like manual signs. Since it can have either kind of function or both at once, neither analysis is accurate nor complete. Moreover it seems also to share, along with certain actions of the hands or modes of action which largely remain outside of descriptions of sig cheremes, a kind of correlating and syntax-signalling function. Facial activity as well as the return of the hands to a resting position can signal a structure's end or the invitation for a reply.

This concentration on the two-channel composition of sign language activity should not be taken to imply any communicative impoverishment by comparison to the normal model of proxemics/kinesics/paralanguage/language. The deaf signer also has at his disposal proxemics and kinesics. The latter will be very much that of the culture in which he is at home, but it is a safe bet that his discriminations of and responses to kinesic signals are more rapid and accurate than the average because of his greater use of visual cues for all messages (personal communication with Ray L. Birdwhistell, 1957). Proxemics understood as interpersonal distance, eye contact, actual physical contact, and other semiotic systems will naturally be different for deaf sign language users. A tap or touch for one who cannot hear does the work of a hail or call between hearing persons, and tactile communication has a larger role in the total communicative activity of deaf persons.

Once it is established that both manual and facial signs are components
of sign language sentences, the question is what each contributes to the
whole structure. If the manual component always supplied the lexical
and grammatical formatives and the facial furnished only overall cues
like 'question', 'assertion', 'negation', 'command', etc., the matter
could be easily settled. But in fact these cues can be supplied as well
by the hands either working in parallel with the face or working alone.
In this there is similarity to the ways that a skillful writer of fiction can
supply much or most of the information that is in a live speaker's
kinesic and paralinguistic performance. More important however is the
division of communicative load in the other direction. Facial phenomena
are not just immanent prosodic features or stylistic additions but may
completely substitute for manual morphemes. To take a generative view,
they may supply a whole portion of the base structure, i.e. the whole
NP or the whole VP branch.

Recognition of this fact can radically change the form of a grammar
of sign language. The first rule in McCall's grammar (1965) rewrites
'sentence' as 'a global gesture' or else as a string consisting of a noun
phrase followed by a verb phrase or of a verb phrase alone:

$$S \rightarrow \begin{Bmatrix} G \\ (NP+)\ VP \end{Bmatrix}$$

But now the question arises whether NP is indeed optional. In all the
sentences the writer has seen NP is not omitted but is realized as a facial
sign. Therefore NP is present as an F component instead of as a manual,
M, component. And whether sign language activity labeled 'G' is
syntactically unanalyzable may also be reexamined. Signs which merely
signal recognition or greeting, 'hi', 'hello', and the like, are clearly
enough unitary; but one sign McCall labels 'G', 'I love you', is indeed
a double manual contraction, utilizing both sign language cheremics and
manual alphabet features. The projection of the little finger is manual
alphabet 'I'. The thumb and index finger form the initial of *love*; and
the thumb and index finger extended are the manual alphabetic 'y',
initial of *you*. Just as 'Didn't' may stand for 'I did not do it', so the
hand with thumb, index, and little fingers may be considered a visual
contraction of *I* and *love (I l')* and of *love* and *you (l' y')*. But while,
unlike an English contraction, it cannot be pronounced, it is put in
performance as an ASL sign. The sig moves it outward from near or
touching the signer's chest (heart) to impart the indexic functions 'I'
and 'love', and toward the addressee — indexic function, 'you'. The

signer keeps the dez vertical, because with entirely different, iconic, force the same dez horizontally used is part of the sign 'fly', 'airplane', 'flight'. With all these functions being contracted into the hand, the signer's face is free to reinforce, modify, or even contradict the semantics of this sign language sentence. Moreover, instead of being an unanalyzed gesture, it is a sentence with a very ordinary structure (Fig. 20).

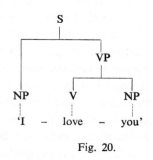

Fig. 20.

Other single sign sentences in the McCall corpus may not be so contracted; but when the facial component is considered, they may really be more complete than an optional first term in the initial rule suggests.

A different kind of grammar seems better adapted to the dual composition of sign language structures. This is the rewriting of S as 'proposition + modality' or 'modality + proposition' (Fillmore, 1968). The problem is to determine which of these two essentially semantic roles the facial component, and which the manual, plays.

While these considerations make linguistic description of sign language more difficult to accomplish than it seemed a decade ago it would be, they do make some kinds of statements easier. Users of handbooks giving sign translations of English words have always been warned that only by observing signers who already know the language can they learn it. Now it is clear that what they must observe after more or less book study of the manual morphemes and their production is the facial component. To this may be added the caution not to expect a close or literal translation to work. The absence of the copula from sign structures and the non-English use and non-use of 'and' have already been referred to as well as the peculiar system of verb auxiliaries. But one who seeks to learn the language will do well to look for facial indications instead of manual indications of the persons of the discourse — or if translating English into sign language, to practice using the face and eyes instead of relying only on manual signs. While this kind of guidance in no way resembles the statements of grammars now in vogue, it is as useful as the information to a hunter in a foreign situation that the quarry he knows only by name is a bird and not a burrowing animal. The analogy is perhaps close enough to remind us that a good deal more rough field hunting, bagging of specimens, and old-fashioned taxonomy needs doing once it is certain that nothing has been missed, before a genuinely generative grammar of American Sign Language can be written.

One area of uncertainty, however, can be ruled out. General treatments of the subject of sign languages or gesture systems contain references to the signs used in monastic communities which have a rule of silence. Perhaps because monasticism is a venerable institution and because medieval, renaissance, and modern attempts to educate deaf persons with signs have been associated with regular or secular clergy, there seems to be a never completely expressed belief that the sign language of monks may be in fact the proto-sign-language. This belief is unfounded.

The examples given of Trappist signing by Barakat (1969) show conclusively that this tradition is a simple substitution code. The message source is an English sentence, presented for translation by the researcher or formulated by the silent signer. The target or coded message is a sign sequence like the ordered pictographs of a rebus. Individual signs and their sequence are intended by the signer and read by the addressee as suggestive of the sound and sense of the source sentence. Barakat reports that Trappists of other nationalities use their native language as source in the same way (p. 116). Thus there is no need for syntax in the code. The signs have only to encode the surface or phonological manifestation of target sentences which have their own syntax. Commonly used words have signs conventionally associated with them for symbols, but terms for objects not encountered inside the walls require a kind of *ad hoc* representation, e.g. *car* is 'machine' or 'drive'- 'machine'. For proper names the monks pun both on the sound of common words and on letter names as in a rebus; e.g. *Milwaukee,* 'milk' - 'walk' - 'key', and *Cincinnati,* 'sin' - 'sin' - *a* - *t* (p. 119). Although Barakat expresses uncertainty about the conventions of alphabetic coding, there can be little doubt that the Trappists use a form of the one-hand manual alphabet familiar in the middle ages (Abernathy, 1959).

Like canting mottoes in heraldry, picture puzzles, and the game of charades, the Trappists' sign code exploits two semiotic properties, signs as icons and signs as indices. Ingenuity in encoding and flexibility in decoding are important when users have no conventional links. The similarity between a Trappist sign and its denotatum, an English word, may be in sound, e.g. signed numerals 'four' and 'two' are used for 'for' and 'to'. It may be in semantic categories, e.g. 'shame'-'house' for 'bathroom'. As an index in this code a sign may point directly to the object signified by a word in the source sentence, or it may point to an object with iconic relation to the denotatum. Semiotically considered this sign system is a surrogate for speech and here has value as a direct contrast with the system of American Sign Language, which is no such thing but which has both its own syntax and a set of meaningless distinctive features — the dual patterning of language.

REFERENCES, CHAPTER 6

Abernathy, Edward R.,
  1959 "An Historical Sketch of the Manual Alphabet", *American Annals of the Deaf* 104, 232-240.
Barakat, Robert A.,
  1969 "Gesture Systems", *Keystone Folklore Quarterly* (Fall), 105-121.
Fillmore, Charles,
  1968 "The Case for Case", *Universals in Linguistic Theory,* ed. by Bach and Harms (New York, Holt).
Gallaudet, T. H.,
  1847 "Two Sign Anecdotes", *American Annuals of the Deaf* 1.
McCall, Elizabeth A.,
  1965 "A Generative Grammar of Sign", M.A. Thesis (University of Iowa).
Stokoe, William C., Jr.,
  1970 "CAL Conference on Sign Language", *Linguistic Reporter* 12:2, 5-8.

7

CURRENT SIGN LANGUAGE RESEARCH

Before 1960 linguists who gave any attention to sign languages supposed that they were speech surrogates. Thus understood, sign languages would have no structure of their own but would preserve more or less of the semantic and syntactic patterning of the language which was physically manifested in signs instead of in speech or writing. Undoubtedly some systems that have been called sign languages do fit this characterization, e.g. the signing of Trappist monks described in Ch. 6.

In *Sign Language Structure* (1960) the writer was able to demonstrate that American Sign Language has both a lexicon of signs denoting the kinds of relations, actions, and things that words denote and a system of cheremes, relatively meaningless, visibly distinguishable, and contrasting collections of features, which combine in language-like ways to compose the morphemes of this lexicon. Skepticism naturally meets a claim that something is a language which is not made of vocal symbols. Skepticism is salutary as well as natural; discovery of a system similar to phonology in a sign language does not settle the question whether that language has a grammar of its own or preserves the syntax of the English used to translate it. For some time after 1960 then, the linguist could still ask whether duality of patterning was an ASL trait; but the question was usually more specific: does American Sign Language have its own grammar?

The appearance of McCall's "Generative Grammar of Sign" (1965), the *Dictionary of American Sign Language* (1965), and other pieces of evidence (Stokoe, 1966; 1970) may not be sufficient to explain the change. Certainly a change in the style and scope of questions asked about language has occurred recently, and the kind of examination and description of phoneme-like sign features made a decade ago is not often done now. At any rate, it is interesting to find young colleagues at linguistics meetings assuming or conceding that American Sign Language has a rule-governed syntactic system while asking whether there is cenemicity, i.e. a level of meaningless symbols or feature bundles. Although the new generation of linguists may assume it, the question whether American Sign Language has a grammar substantially similar to that of other languages has not been settled. Assuming that it has is not the same thing as describing the grammar. Besides, the statements made about ASL syntax range from denial that there is any such system to claims that it is but the syntax of English or that it is part of the general non-verbal behavior of zoosemiotics. These statements indicate the difficulty and confusion encountered in any search for an accurate description of sign language syntax.

Other questions are entailed by the central one. Does American Sign Language belong to a single, universal class, language? Has it therefore a system in which abstract syntactic generation precedes semantic and expressive interpretations of the generated structures? Whether the last question has a negative or affirmative answer, is the priority of syntax over semantics and phonology a universal of language? And what of a hierarchy of structures? Can ASL syntax be described by looking at morpheme structure, i.e. are there form classes or such categories as Determiner, Noun, Verb, and Adverb in this language?

One point is clear. Approaches to a description of ASL syntax must begin from that language. Schlesinger (1969), Cicourel and Boese (1971), and others since Mallery (1881) have taken all communicative activity involving gesture apart from speech as sign language. Others interested in sign language as a test case for generative theory seem to define it as an infinite set of sentences generated by a finite set of rules operating on a lexicon of morphemes which are manifested visibly instead of vocally. Cicourel (1969: 27ff) seems to incline toward the latter view, and McCall (1965) uses a corpus of conversations in sign (her term) between deaf persons at a picnic to be generated by the rules she writes. Beginning from the language requires sociological and practical as well as theoretical preliminaries. American Sign Language is the language used by most deaf Americans. It has close relation to French Sign Language which is first described in Épée (1776), having been imported by a native signer of the latter, Laurent Clerc, in 1817. It is not used by all deaf Americans, though the number of adults whose deafness dates from childhood or adolescence and who do not sign is very small. Most signers of American Sign Language learn it later than the usual age for first language acquisition. This is because only the children (hearing as well as deaf) of deaf, signing parents have the same opportunity as hearing children of hearing parents to grow up knowing their native language. Most signers have begun to acquire American Sign Language at six or seven years of age when they first attended school, often a residential institution, where being surrounded by signers they 'picked it up' as naturally as hearing children learn to use second language when the family moves into another culture. More recently the population increase and the expansion of day schools and classes for deaf children have worked to delay the age of sign language acquisition for many. The divided home-school environment usually offers less opportunity for natural and frequent use of signs. An increasing number, and it may be a somewhat larger proportion, of deaf students are coming to Gallaudet College without a knowledge of signs (or fingerspelling) and acquire the language in formal classes as well as in informal interaction. The situation is changing, then, but it is still not comparable to that in Britain where deaf children are educated in oral schools leave at fourteen or fifteen and often achieve neither identity, social stability nor economic viability, until after five or six years of drifting they overcome earlier conditioning, make contact with the non-oral deaf social groups, learn the sign language, and enter the society of deaf adults (Gorman, 1960).

Again not all users of American Sign Language can understand each other. Although cherology and lexicon and other features may show their sign dialects to be ASL dialects, a rural southern black and an urban northern white signer may find each others' sign sentences unintelligible. This is not entirely a function of structural difference in their ASL dialects, however. Other factors being equal, the more a signer's dialect or idiolect is contaminated by his knowledge and use of fingerspelled or spoken English, the more it will diverge from a relatively purer ASL dialect. Nevertheless there is a remarkable high degree of mutual intelligibility throughout the United States, Canada, and those parts of Mexico geographically or culturally close to the states. This is not at all the case in other English-speaking regions. The sign language of a deaf group centered in Canterbury was studied by the writer for six weeks in 1961 but was of little use in communicating with deaf persons in other parts of Britain so that most communication had to be with English words spelled with the two-hand alphabet. Across the Irish Sea communication with deaf adults in Dublin and boys in St. Joseph's School, Cabra, was easier because they used a one-hand alphabet for fingerspelling with only three or four configuration differences from that in use in the U.S. and also because some of their signs were cognate with ASL signs. The term cognate is used in its comparative philological sense. Just as ASL users are the inheritors of a language and a signer imported from France in 1817, the school at Cabra, operated by the Christian Brothers, grew from a nuclear religious community sent out from France. American Sign Language and Irish Sign Language both stem from French Sign Language.

This digression from the linguistic community of American Sign Language obviously gives the lie to all who claim that there is but one sign language understood by all who sign (i.e. deaf persons, red Indians, Neapolitans, or anyone that the observer has noticed using numerous gestures). It has a corollary too. The writer had acquired enough ASL competence in six years to find in 1961 no difficulty whatever conversing with deaf signers in Paris, though he has no command of spoken French and most of them had no knowledge of English. The reason ASL signers and British SL signers cannot communicate easily while ASL signers and FSL signers can is precisely analogous to the reasons monolingual Britons and Americans can converse while Americans and French cannot. It is recognition of linguistic history and geography of this order that must precede theoretical and practical attempts to describe 'sign language'. To cook a hare, first catch the hare. Nevertheless a great deal of what has been written about sign language resembles hare soup that has boiled long while the hare was still afield.

What has been observed and exaggerated or misunderstood that lends credence to treatment of sign language as a natural universal human possession is that persons who habitually use signs, such as deaf persons, seem to speaking observers to make contact, get along, and reach communicative efficiency in a shorter time than would be needed by two speakers of different languages. For real understanding, even when the two sign users are ASL signers, more or less time will be required; and the variables on which communicative efficiency depend include their relative age, sex, education, bilingual experience, environment, and temperament as well as the usual vertical or social and horizontal or geographical separation of their dialects.

It should be clearly understood, then, that the present approach to a description of ASL grammar starts from these prelinguistic determinations: First, American Sign Language is a sign language, one of possibly many sign languages. Second, while its signers are mutually intelligible to each other, there are various degrees of intelligibility, many dialects, and a great many idiolects (possibly a quarter of a million) of this language. Third, a description of the language, or a grammar of the language, must not be of any one idiolect or dialect but must be general enough to account for all.

What a number of psycholinguistic studies have not taken into account is what has just been reviewed. If sign language were a uniform, homogeneous, and well ordered system throughout the ASL population (or as some assume throughout the total population that signs), then statistical and sampling procedures to secure subjects informants would be valid. But American Sign Language has no such uniformity, and the selection of informants for its study calls for as much care as is exercised in any linguistic research — indeed more care, for ASL is nowhere found in isolation so that the linguist is forced to consider its relation, inside the informant, to the other language, American English, in the same community.

Early in the research an ideal informant was thought of as an intelligent, adult, fully enculturated member of the ASL community who used little or no English. Such an informant was never found, of course. One mark of an intelligent adult signer is the competence he has in the language surrounding him. This is not to say he must be proficient in lipreading (intelligence and lipreading skills are often negatively correlated) nor skillful in producing audible and intelligible speech. It is instead to understand that he has competence in the semological and morphological systems of English which he uses, not through phonology, but through fingerspelling as well as through the conventional writing system of a literate technological culture. One must then settle for a bilingual informant. American Sign Language is an exotic language, in some ways as remote from speakers of American English as proto-Papuan and until very recently less well known to the community of language scientists; but while it remains strange to those who do not have cause to use it, its users must participate fully in the general culture and within the limits already defined in the language of the general population.

Lacking the intelligent adult monolingual ASL informant in touch with all that surrounds him, the linguist may find a relatively monolingual signer. This one will use little English, for he may have had no school experience. However the kind of isolation which can prevent a deaf child from getting any formal education in the present American scene is likely also to preclude contact with ASL users. Therefore this signer if found is elderly and has a minimum of contact with neighbors as well as with the outside world. His signs are of interest to the ASL lexicographer; though it is a problem to determine whether they are survivals from an older dialect or coinages in an idiolect. And while he may use some signs not found in other research, his sign vocabulary is necessarily much limited by his lack of contact with other signers.

Since an intelligent enculturated adult ASL informant is by these very qualities obliged to be bilingual, the nature and kind of bias that bilingualism may introduce into a study of sign language is of concern. For a hearing researcher the informant who also hears and speaks the researcher's language greatly facilitates proceedings. But few if any hearing persons acquire true native competence in American Sign Language. The native signer who can hear is the child of deaf parents who use American Sign Language in the family without constraint. But this stipulation is not always met. In their natural concern for their child's welfare deaf parents may change their language habits or show a reluctance to use sign language when the child's hearing friends are present. A different bias comes from the informant who has at a very early age been thrust into the role of interpreter between the spoken English and the sign language of his environment. But even if the child in the home never encounters negative attitudes toward sign language, his experiences in the hearing world, in school and out, are likely to produce in the adult bilingual informant conscious and subconscious bias against the language of signs. If he or she enters the educational system for the deaf, the anti-sign-language bias is developed into a full system of prejudice buttressed by specious scientism. The bilingual become interpreter become authority will insist that the language of signs is agrammatical, that it is a beautiful and expressive language, that a given utterance cannot be translated into it but must be fingerspelled, and that deaf people who sign ... but here the individual experience completely controls and the judgment expressed may be highly favorable or totally condemnatory or unresolvedly ambivalent.

Quite clearly an informant for the study of the language is not to be found among these, however useful they may be as subjects for social and psychological research. If the ideal native-signer, native-speaker kind of bilingual informant is not a hearing child of deaf signing parents, the choice then falls on those persons who are born deaf, who acquire ASL competence in the most natural way from parents and from living much among other deaf people, who use their sign language among themselves whatever their public attitudes toward it in the outer world, and who also achieve native or near native competence in English. This set of conditions is not easily met. Explicitly or tacitly, the educational system for the deaf is dedicated to instilling competence in English by denying or extirpating sign language competence. The usual fate of deaf children of deaf parents is to acquire the label 'oral failures' and early in their school experience to be put on a vocational track terminating in a semi-skilled trade (Kohl, 1966). Those fortunate ones who escape had parents themselves bilingual and learned English (fingerspelled and book-printed) before going to school (see Ch. 8). Even these fortunate few, however, cannot escape the effect of twelve to sixteen or more years in educational institutions nor contact with persons hearing and deaf who denigrate sign language.

A prejudice against the language used is not unusual in informants or whole linguistic communities (Ferguson, 1953; Stokoe, 1970); and it does not interfere with elicitation of data from informants to use in cherological analysis of American Sign Language. When the linguist turns to the morpheme inventory, however, it may inhibit data gathering. Asked how something would be put in signs, an informant carefully selected, with the foregoing cautions observed, still may say: "There isn't a sign; spell it". But it may happen that the investigator will later encounter a sign in use which exactly fits. If he asks the original informant, the answer may be: "Oh, yes; that's a slang sign; some people use it". Knowing such attitudes exist, the compiler of the lexicon can take suitable steps to minimize error.

But when the center of attention shifts from the cheremic system and the lexicon to the syntactic system, the nature and importance of informant error changes. Signs as translations for words are easily elicited as are signs for objects pointed to or signs for relations and situations supplied by the usual ploys of the linguistic investigator. The cheremes of the signs so elicited may then be examined without arousing self-consciousness. The morphemes of sign language are also accessible as long as care is taken to ensure that the informant is not screening out or holding back signs not judged suitable for consultative performance. Sign sentences, however, will almost always be elicited in these conditions as English sentences with signs as surrogates for words; and so a different kind of informant is required.

The progressively selective criteria for selection of informants so far have been: *ex natu* deafness and exposure to ASL use, early English language competence, intelligence, maturity (because children's language differs from adolescents' language differs from adults' language in all cultures), full enculturation, and trust in the investigator not to assume superiority or betray confidence when given esoteric material. Although the size of the group selected thus is very small, these criteria are not enough because even such informants will still both consciously and unconsciously operate their English syntax generating internal machinery instead of its ASL counterpart except in purely ASL situations which linguistic research plainly is not.

The final essential step in selection of an informant is to employ a negative criterion. One who meets all the tests above must then be free of all bias preferring English to ASL syntax. Such a qualification is not natural, given the active formal, informal, and technical teaching in the other direction. So in fact the only suitable informant is not found but formed. One with all the other characteristics described who has studied linguistics and anthropology, who has practiced making analyses and writing rules, and who has come to see which statements encountered are the statements of linguistic science and which are the idols of the marketplace, makes not simply an ideal informant but actually the only reliable informant for a study of ASL syntax.

The necessity of selecting and by training forming an informant suitable for sign language research has only lately been recognized and the process is still going forward; nevertheless it already has provided an unusual point of vantage for viewing current research in sign language.

The work of I. M. Schlesinger, Jonathan Shunary, and Tisona Peled of the Department of Psychology, Hebrew University of Jerusalem, deals with Israeli Sign Language. From their reports, it appears to be a recent and mixed or creolized sign language (Shunary, 1969). Those who use it are deaf persons who have come to the Tel Aviv area from many parts of Europe and who have used a number of dissimilar sign languages before emigrating to Israel. One of the most interesting features of this language is its newness: it has grown in the close-knit community using it from many branches or roots probably not connected to the same language stock. It is also unusual in working without a parallel system of fingerspelling; the signers apparently prefer to do without a manual alphabet since use of one would require or else pretend that all the members of the deaf community in Tel Aviv know Hebrew or some other common tongue (1969: p. 3). An even more interesting aspect of Israeli Sign Language is reported by Schlesinger (1969): it seems to have no regular means of indicating such important syntactic points as subject, verb, object, and indirect object. What in fact Schlesinger reports is that when a number of subjects who use Israeli Sign Language were given a familiar psycholinguistic task, the results were incompatible with the hypothesis that Israeli Sign Language uses relative and absolute order of signs to indicate the syntactic units. He concludes that no regular order can be seen in the responses elicited, a small proportion of which were judged to be complete sentences, but is unwilling to concede that this sign language is therefore without a grammar. As he points out, none of the subjects, whatever the lack of grammaticality of their sign responses, is unaware of the difference between, e.g., the man gave the boy a bear and the bear gave the boy a man.

Three points may help explain the equivocal results of this look at Israeli Sign Language; two of them are found in the design of the experiment, and in many other experiments with deaf children, and the other comes from the perspective of the present review. First, the use of pictures in psycholinguistic experiments has dangers. If one could be certain that subjects and experimenters share not only a common language but also a common culture and detailed sub-culture, one might have more confidence that subjects looking at the pictures see and understand the things, ideas, and actions that the experimenter confidently describes. This is a condition, however, not often met. The classic example of cross-cultural difference in response to pictorial representation is that given by Lawrence in *Seven Pillars of Wisdom*: Arab nomads had no idea of what his sketch of their sheikh was; asked to say what it looked like, one ventured the guess that it was a foot! Children in American culture who have gone through several years of reading from books with frequent pictures and dialogue in which the word *look* seems most prominent are likely to be able to read a picture as readily as a line of text (Is it coincidence that in many of the pictures used in this kind of psycholinguistic research the style and content seem to come from the same books?). A very strong argument can be made that native signers, i.e. children who have not had the same linguistic and hence cultural experiences as native speakers, not only 'see' different things in the pictures but also 'say' different things are happening in them. Even this is too close to the usual cultural pattern to be accurate. More likely is that deaf children used to watching action, of faces, of hands and fingers, of total participation, think something is happening when live people are observed, but that in still pictures, photographs or 'Look, Dick, look!' drawings, nothing at all is happening. Thus, whether the subject has to respond by telling another what he sees in the picture or by choosing the correct caption for the picture, the experimental variable may be considerably different from what it is assumed to be, the competence of the subject in sign language or in English.

The second point to be considered in connection with Schlesinger's attempt to elicit from subject's responses the surface grammatical structure of Israeli Sign Language is the state of that language itself. From Shunary's brief history of the community, it appears that communication in signs is now taking place and has been doing so for some time among a very mixed population, young and old, well-educated and without any formal schooling, literate in one or more European languages and Hebrew and completely illiterate; the members of the group have not acquired a language already extant but have hammered out a *modus operandi* in less than one generation. One may wonder whether this sign language indeed has a regular grammar or is instead but a few stages from the kind of *ad hoc* gesture communication indulged in by anyone who finds himself on the wrong side of a language barrier.

There is a third point to consider before becoming too skeptical of the linguistic status of Israeli Sign Language. It may be true that it is recent of development, that it is formed by selection and synthesis from several sign languages instead of by evolution from one, and that by refusing to introduce fingerspelling its users have deliberately kept it out of direct contact with a recognized language with all its structural regularity. However, the intuition of Schlesinger that the users of that sign language do understand each other and do deal unambiguously with structures at least as complex as those in S-V-O-IO sentences should be heeded. Schlesinger, like everyone who has dealt with sign languages, tends to think of signs as uninflected absolutes. Now, if signs are in fact uninflected, then the only way for syntactic structure to be shown in strings of signs is by the order of signs in the strings. The most sophisticated statistical procedures could not show regularity of order in his subjects' responses; hence the doubt that they were using a language with even elementary syntax; nevertheless their behavior outside the experiment indicates understanding of such things.

Much becomes clear if it is understood that sign language, at least American Sign Language, is inflected in the same sense that *play* and *house* are inflected in the following two sentences: (1) *Let's play house.* (2) *It's a playhouse.* There are no suffixes to show number or to show tense, but the stress, juncture, and pitch generation in the performance of each of the English sentences signal very clearly the difference in syntax, a difference that a hearing child in kindergarten is perfectly competent to appreciate. Similarly in sign language, there are none of the paradigmatic trappings of inflection, but there is always the signer's body, all of it not involved in producing the lexical sign, to indicate motion, direction, connection, and disjunction. The conclusion is clear.

Just as future investigations of ASL grammar must consider very carefully what it is that makes the same sign now a verb now a noun when order alone cannot account for it, so the examination of Israeli Sign Language needs to include a wider view of what happens when signers in Tel Aviv communicate.

A different approach to sign language investigation is taken by Cicourel and Boese (1971). In "Sign Language Acquisition and the Teaching of Deaf Children" they discuss the matter of the linguistic competence of persons born deaf. Whether the child has deaf parents or hearing parents, they contend, his first symbolic treatment of experience, i.e. his native language, is bound to be visual, sign language or quasi-sign language. His later acquisition of lip reading skill and speech production, no matter how proficient he becomes, will be related to his native language competence, because lacking the means of self-monitoring the second language he cannot achieve a native speaker's or a coordinate bilingual's control of its syntactic, semantic, and phonological systems. Cicourel treats also the nature of a signer's competence (1968) as part of his theory of a developmental sociology of language and meaning. This has to do with a deep structure of social interaction shared by persons who communicate and a surface structure of language which has an 'indexical' function. There is much more to the theory of course than can be indicated in this brief view, but it seems to accord well with the results of this writer's study of sign language. Interchanges in all languages contain expressions that refer to the social situation occasioned by speakers in contact, but the linguistic signs (the 'surface structure' as Cicourel calls it) point to only a part of the whole social complex (deep structure) that participants in any meaningful exchange must have acquired.

The recommendations for teachers of deaf children that Cicourel and Boese make are also in keeping with those of Kohl (1966) and the research on sign language centered in Gallaudet College, but one difference in terminology should be noted. Cicourel and Boese refer to 'American sign language' as distinct from 'native sign language' in a way which indicates that the first is what this writer and others call 'Signed English' and the second American Sign Language in the L form of a diglossic pair (Stokoe, 1970). There is in fact more than a terminological difference. When the approach is from linguistics, the system called here American Sign Language is seen to include an entire spectrum with signed English at one end and a very un-English sign structure at the other. Separate from this would be the various minor sign languages invented for their own use by small groups of deaf persons isolated from contact with ASL users. When the approach is from Cicourel's theory of sociology, the separation is between those who have competence in any language like English and those who use any sign language at all. The implications for the teacher are the same with either approach: deaf children acquiring literacy and speaking and lipreading ability do not handle a second language in the same way as hearing children who must acquire another language. But for the teacher and for those who will do the research needed it may be important to distinguish ASL dialects and the language itself from *ad hoc* sign conventions and ephemeral gestural codes.

An entirely different kind of sign language research has added a number of new signs to the lexicon of American Sign Language. It may be called psycholinguistic because the new signs were introduced to selected signing subjects who were tested on retention of each new sign and recognition of its meaning. More interesting to the linguist who studies sign language as a natural language is the extent to which new signs coined and introduced during the project are being encountered in use among persons who were not directly involved in the testing a year or two after the introduction of the signs. The research is also encyclopedic: fifteen academic departments participated cooperatively in determining what additions to the lexicon of ASL signs were needed for pedagogy in their fields of knowledge. The whole project is reported in Bornstein and Kannapell (1969), and the signs, are shown in pictures and described in drawings in Kannapell, Hamilton, and Bornstein (1969). The foreword of the latter book is quoted in full below:

This book depicts 465 new signs intended for use in instruction in high school and college. Each sign represents a word or phrase important to a subject matter, used frequently in class, and usually made up of many letters. We believe that use of these signs will enable the signer to communicate with deaf persons more quickly and more precisely.

The signs are the outcome of a three year effort by the Office of Institutional Research and the faculty of Gallaudet College. The work was partially supported by Grant OEG 2-6-061924-1890 from the Bureau of Education for the Handicapped, U.S. Office of Education, HEW.

The terms for which signs were invented were nominated by Gallaudet faculty. Sign invention followed five basic rationales, namely: (1) an existing sign with a letter cue, (2) a compound of two existing signs, (3) a compound of a letter and an existing sign, (4) a completely new sign, and (5) a new sign with letter cue. In addition, consultants created a small number of signs "spontaneously", i.e. without any construction guide.

Each new sign was judged for its clarity and appearance. Only those judged good or excellent on both attributes were used in classrooms.

It was found that the new signs were easily learned by students. After the signs were used in class for one year, the faculty made suggestions for revisions, deletions, and additions. The revised signs were used for a second year before being accepted for inclusion in this book.

Complete details on the development and evaluation of these signs can be found in the report listed below:

> Bornstein, H., and Kannapell, B., *Report on New Signs for Instructional Purposes*. O.E. Project 6-1924, October 1969.

Recent writing[1] on the sign language used by deaf persons in the Soviet Union reflects the national policy in special education and social services. Marcinovskaja (1969) gives a brief history which connects early Russian teaching of the deaf and dumb to the French school: the first Russian school was opened at Pavlosk in 1806 by A. Sigmund, a Roman Catholic priest who studied under I. Maj and F. Stork, pupils of Épée; in 1810 the school was moved to nearby St. Petersburg and came under the direction of I. A. Žoffre, a former student of Siccard. She also summarizes information from the first book published in Russia on the training and upbringing of the deaf and dumb (Fleri, 1835). It includes a lithograph of the Russian manual alphabet, based on the one used in France, but with 32 letters instead of 26. Her research concerns speed of recognition of lipreading and fingerspelling (respectively 300 'znacks' a minute versus 350), and she concludes that fingerspelling is helpful in the beginning of the deaf pupil's training. An earlier article by Marcinovskaja (1964) relies heavily on Best (1943) and adds little on the history of the use of the manual alphabet in Russia to the outline in her 1969 article.

S. A. Zykov (1965) writing on the "Sign Language" sees it as a distinctive form of communication using expressive movements of the face and hands, the former contributing mimicry or 'natural expressions' and the latter, signs, characterized by concreteness. He calls the signs ideographic and estimates the number at 2,500 to 3,000, or one one-hundredth of the Russian vocabulary. Like earlier writers on the American Sign Language, he finds signs lacking in morphology, prefixes, suffixes, and endings, e.g. 'labor', 'to labor', and 'laboring' (adj) are all the same sign, as are 'cold' and 'to be afraid'. He notes that the

---

[1] I am indebteded to Charles H. Yeager, Associate Professor of Russian, Gallaudet College, for summaries and references in this section. His search and translation of sources makes possible for the first time the identification of Russian Sign Language as a cognate language with American Sign Language.

usual syntactic order is subject, object, and verb, a structure common enough in American Sign Language and agreeing with some examples of early French natural signs.

The fullest source of information on Russian signs is that by I. F. Gejl'man (1957). It is a descriptive dictionary of the sign language (alphabetic arrangement of Russian words, verbal description of sign production, and photographs). It also has an informative introduction (incompletely translated by Joseph and Tunya Ziv, 1964). In it he notes that "Of the 70 gesture signs described by Fleri in 1835 in his book ... 75% of the gesture signs remained unchanged and are utilized at the present time, 22.5% of the gestures changed their character but still can be understood even in our day, and only 2.5% of the gestures are no longer in use or took on a different meaning" (1964: 72). There is an interesting difference between Gejl'man's work and that of the writers reviewed just above. They are concerned with pedagogic policies in the teaching of language (Russian) to deaf children, while he is concerned with the social programs for the deaf population and connected with the All Russian Society of Deaf Mutes. Apparently in Russia as in England and in the United States educational psychology changes sufficiently from time to time to effect major differences in the direction of language pedagogy for the deaf, but the stable population of deaf persons (about one in one thousand of an entire population) as a sign-linguistic community exhibits all the characteristics of users of any natural language.

Besides noting recent research in this chapter it is possible to incorporate some. James C. Woodward, Jr., Gallaudet College, has investigated several relations between the surface structure of ASL sentences and deeper, more universal syntax. The writer is grateful to him for permission to quote in full his paper, "A Transformational Approach to the Syntax of American Sign Language".

A TRANSFORMATIONAL APPROACH TO THE SYNTAX OF AMERICAN SIGN LANGUAGE

James Clyde Woodward, Jr.
Gallaudet College

Chomsky (1969) has stated that a synthesis of philosophical and descriptive grammar is justifiable and desirable. Not only must we attempt to describe what actually occurs in the specific language under investigation, but we should try to relate our findings to a universal theory of language. Such a universal theory perhaps will help us discover some insights into language and mental processes.

Since language is used for communicating ideas, it is obvious that grammar is no more than a code for arranging these ideas for expression. But all languages share some common basis for choosing their specific codes. Otherwise, how can we classify all languages under the same heading — language? This common basis may be called the general deep structure or language universals, and the language specific codes may be called surface structure, which also contains deeper elements than are necessarily expressed in the final output of speech.

Languages such as American Sign Language may give us some invaluable insights into this commonly shared deep structure of languages. For American Sign Language seems to have relatively little of what we normally think of as surface structure. There are ordering rules that may be applied, but there seem to be few if any actual inflections. Transformations other than questions, negatives, and commands seem to function only to emphasize a particular item. The signs themselves are affected little by surface structure restrictions.

What surface structure there is is largely manifested in the facial expression and body movement accompanying the signs. Facial expression in vocal language is paralinguistic or kinesic. However, in the visual communication of Sign Language, facial expression and body movement serve as intonation and some syntactic allomorphs, such as using shaking of the head as an allomorph of $\cup \dot{A}^{\perp}$ 'not'. Exactly what part the face and the body play in American Sign Language is not understood yet. Therefore, this paper will concentrate on the syntactic relationships between signs. Facial expression and body movements will be mentioned only occasionally, but it should be kept in mind that these two elements can and do function in the grammar of American Sign Language.

Basically, this paper attempts to show some sentences in American Sign Language that are determined by few, if any, surface restrictions and that perhaps may be representations of the deep structure of languages in general. Efforts are made to analyze these sentences according to a modified case grammar and semantic analysis and to relate the results to a more general theory of the structure of language.

One article that comes to sociolinguistic grips with American Sign Language is William Stokoe's "Sign Language Diglossia" (1970). In the paper, Stokoe takes Ferguson's (1959) nine features of diglossia and applies these features to American Sign Language. The High (H) variety of signs is 'Signed English'. This is a combination of signs and finger-spelling (sometimes only fingerspelling) that follows the grammatical structure of English. The Low (L) variety uses little or no fingerspelling and follows a different grammatical structure.

H is used in formal conversation, such as in church, the classroom, lectures, etc. L is used in smaller, less formal, more intimate conversa-tions. H is considered superior to L, and L is regarded as ungrammatical or non-existent. L is learned by a very young child only if he has deaf parents. If the child has hearing parents, he will learn L only when he goes to school and contacts other deaf children his age.

Deaf signers generally feel that 'grammatical' H should be used instead of L for teaching. Some feel that standardization of L is neces-sary, but sign language diglossia appears as stable as other diglossic situations.

And although L's grammatical system is much simpler than H's, much of the vocabulary of H and L are shared. Finally, the gestemic (comparable to phonological) systems of H (fingerspelling and signs) and L (signs) constitute a single basic system. The differences of the H gestemic system can be considered a subsystem of L or a parasystem of L.

For the purpose of an initial linguistic description, this dichotomy of H and L may be retained for the sake of clarity. Linguistic descrip-tions are always abstractions and so this dichotomy is acceptable.

However, in actual conversation, depending on the social situation and educational background of the speakers, there may be a mixing of H and L. The mixing will not be considered in this paper, but should be incorporated into a later more comprehensive work, perhaps using principles outlined by Edward Klima in "Relatedness Between Gram-matical Systems" (1969).

It should be noted that from now on in this paper when the term American Sign Language is used, only the Low variety is meant.

A unique orthographic representation of signs has been devised by Stokoe; according to this (1965: vii) the sign is composed of at least three basic components: the tab or place where the sign is made, the dez or the distinctive configuration of the hand or hands making the sign, and the sig, or the action of the hand or hands. In the orthographic convention, the tab is written first, followed by the dez and sig. Some signs may be produced with a combination of two tabs, dezes, or sigs. This is also denoted by the orthography. A "Table of Symbols used for Writing the Signs of American Sign Language" (Stokoe, 1965: x-xii,

Table of symbols used for writing the signs of the American sign language

Tab symbols

1. Ø   zero, the neutral place where the hands move, in contrast with all places below
2. Ọ   face or whole head
3. ∩   forehead or brow, upper face
4. ப   mid-face, the eye and nose region
5. ∪   chin, lower face
6. }   cheek, temple, ear, side-face
7. π   neck
8. []   trunk, body from shoulders to hips
9. \   upper arm
10. ✓   elbow, forearm
11. ᗩ   wrist, arm in supinated position (on its back)
12. ᗪ   wrist, arm in pronated position (face down)

Dez symbols, some also used as tab

13. A   compact hand, fist; may be like 'a', 's', or 't' of manual alphabet
14. B   flat hand
15. 5   spread hand; fingers and thumb spread like '5' of manual numeration
16. C   curved hand; may be like 'c' or more open
17. E   contracted hand; like 'e' or more clawlike
18. F   "three-ring" hand; from spread hand, thumb and index finger touch or cross
19. G   index hand; like 'g' or sometimes like 'd'; index finger points from fist
20. H   index and second finger, side by side, extended
21. I   "pinkie" hand; little finger extended from compact hand
22. K   like G except that thumb touches middle phalanx of second finger; like 'k' and 'p' of manual alphabet
23. L   angle hand; thumb, index finger in right angle, other fingers usually bent into palm
24. 3   "cock" hand; thumb and first two fingers spread, like '3' of manual numeration
25. O   tapered hand; fingers curved and squeezed together over thumb; may be like 'o' of manual alphabet
26. R   "warding off" hand; second finger crossed over index finger, like 'r' of manual alphabet

Fig. 1

27. V "victory" hand; index and second fingers extended and spread apart
28. W three-finger hand; thumb and little finger touch, others extended spread
29. X hook hand; index finger bent in hook from fist, thumb tip may touch fingertip
30. Y "horns" hand; thumb and little finger spread out extended from fist; or index finger and little finger extended, parallel
31. 8 (allocheric variant of Y); second finger bent in from spread hand, thumb may touch fingertip

Sig symbols

32. ^ upward movement
33. v downward movement   } vertical action
34. N up-and-down movement
35. > rightward movement
36. < leftward movement   } sideways action
37. z side to side movement
38. T movement toward signer
39. ⊥ movement away from signer } horizontal action
40. I to-and-fro movement
41. ɑ supinating rotation (palm up)
42. ᴅ pronating rotation (palm down) } rotary action
43. ɯ twisting movement
44. ŋ nodding or bending action
45. □ opening action (final dez configuration shown in brackets)
46. # closing action (final dez configuration shown in brackets)
47. ⋏ wiggling action of fingers
48. ᴑ circular action
49.)(convergent action, approach
50. × contactual action, touch
51. ⊞ linking action, grasp
52. ✝ crossing action   } interaction
53. ⊙ entering action
54. ÷ divergent action, separate
55. (,) interchanging action

Fig. 1

and end of paper) is given in Fig. 1. All examples in this paper will first
be written in this orthography, followed by a literal word for word
translation into English, followed by the equivalent of the sentence in
English.

Bruner (1968) has stated that he believes that the idea of predication
(topic and comment) in human language is a universal of language that
is evolutionary in origin. He believes that topicizing involves the same
basic diffuse capabilities as the ability to hold an object in one hand
and that commenting involves the same basic focal capabilities as the
ability to operate on an object with the other hand.

In American Sign Language, the three basic topic-comment types that
Bruner mentions are present.

$$\cap 5_v^\perp \qquad \triangle V_T^\perp \qquad 3\dot{A}\bar{x}^\perp \phi B_v{}^V$$

	man	see		girl
The	man	sees	the	girl

$$\cap 5_v^\perp \qquad\qquad XX^{\pi}$$

	man			friend
The	man	is	my	friend

$$\cap 5_a^\perp \qquad \cup^V B_T^\perp$$

	man		good
The	man	is	good

The structure of these sentences could be explained by the following
rules.

S → Topic   Comment
Topic → NP
Comment → $\begin{Bmatrix} V & NP \\ NP \\ Adj \end{Bmatrix}$

Tree diagrams can be drawn to graphically demonstrate the application of the rules:

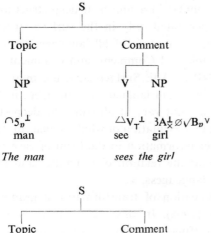

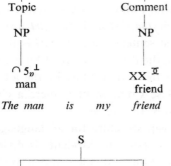

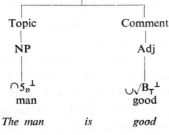

The adjective in sentence three has been considered a verbal with /—V/ characteristics as opposed to the /+V/ of *see*. However, sentences such as *The man is my friend* have been considered (Jacobs and Rosenbaum, 1968) as special types of transitive sentences with the verb *be*, as a special type of transitive verb. This is not true of American Sign Language. There is never a copula between NP and NP or between NP and Adj, so these sentences cannot be considered as having come from a verbal deletion transformational rule.

The best way to handle copulas in a universal deep structure theory is to consider them to be generated only in the surface structures of specific languages. In the deep structure of all languages there is only this relationship between Topic and Comment, and Comment does not imply VP alone, but also NP or Adj. Surface structure manifestations of this deep structure will vary from language to language; in fact, the actual surface production may not vary at all from the deep structure.

Although this is an accurate presentation of what happens in American Sign Language, some further information in the form of case grammar will provide more insight into the relation of semantics and syntax in signs and perhaps in other languages.

Case grammar is a modification of transformational grammar proposed by Charles Fillmore (1968). In this theory, there is a division between deep structure case (function) and surface structure case. For example, in the sentences *Paul saw the girl* and *The girl was seen by Paul*, *Paul* is the subject of the first sentence and *the girl* is the subject of the second sentence. However, in the deep structure of both sentences, *Paul* is the Agent or person doing the action. Only by the addition of a passive transformation in the Base Component is there a change in the surface structure representation of the Agent.

Fillmore proposes that in the deep structure for all languages there is a Modality (M) and a Proposition (P). The Modality is divided into tense, aspect, etc.; and the Proposition is divided into a verb and a number of case categories, such as: Agent (animate actor), Object (neutral inanimate), Instrument (inanimate instrument), etc.

Fillmore lists at least six basic cases and says that there are probably more. However, Fillmore's model cases do not all seem to be applicable to American Sign Language, e.g. the Instrument. In the English sentence *John broke the window with a hammer*, *hammer* is the instrument. However, in signs, there is no Instrument in the equivalent sentence in signs nor in any similar sentence.

j.o.h.n	$\phi\,A^{\mathrm{I}\cdot}$	$A_v{}^{\prime}A_{v\dotplus}{}^{a}$	$\bar{B}_>B_<{}^{\times\cdot}$
John	hammer	broke	window

j.o.h.n	$A_v{}^{\prime}A_{v\dotplus}{}^{a}$	$\bar{B}_>B_<{}^{\times\cdot}$	$\phi\,A^{\mathrm{I}\cdot}$
John	broke	window	hammer

Hammer in both these sentences may be looked upon as a conjoined or embedded VP (see below).

Although Fillmore's noun category, Instrument, does not appear in signs, his basic idea of applying semantic features to explain certain syntactical constructions and restrictions deserves special attention. It is a possibility that Fillmore's cases are not as deep as we can go, but are actually clues to a deeper structure. This idea of a semantic interpretation of syntactical restrictions will be developed further in the following section.

McCawley (1968) mentions sentences such as *My sister is the father of two* as violations of semantic selectional restrictions. There are more general semantic selectional restrictions that can and do apply in languages. For example, *The television ate the food* is a violation of normal semantic choices. *Eating* is an action that has to be related to an animate being, an Agent.

Goldin (1968: 12) states that "in the deep structure the function of the subject and the object is to restrict the choice of verb". To the writer, the statement as it stands is not true, but its converse is true. Verbs like *eat* cannot take an inanimate noun (Fillmore's Object) as a surface subject, but verbs such as *open* can take an animate (Agent) or an inanimate (Object) as the surface subject. It is the semantic properties of the verb that determine whether an animate or inanimate noun is chosen as the subject. And it is the non-use of a verb that makes it possible to make sentences with two animate or inanimate noun phrases.

Therefore, verbs should be marked as to whether they are +animate or —animate. The feature +animate means that an animate noun must occur as the subject of the sentence; —animate means that either an animate noun (Agent) or an inanimate noun (Object) can be chosen. If the animate noun is chosen, the inanimate noun becomes the object on the surface, otherwise the inanimate noun may become the subject on the surface. Lack of a verb will imply ±animate. Rules may be formulated to describe this phenomena.

$$\begin{array}{ccccc} NP & V & \Rightarrow & NP & V \\ /\propto\text{animate}/ & /+\text{animate}/ & & /+\text{animate}/ & /\propto\text{animate}/ \end{array}$$

Another (optional) rule is necessary.

$$\begin{array}{ccccc} V & NP & \Rightarrow & NP & V \\ -\text{animate} & -\text{animate} & & -\text{animate} & -\text{animate} \\ +\text{object} & & & & +\text{object} \end{array}$$

(where animate topic is deleted)

These rules will give us the following possibilities:

	$\cap 5_a{}^{\perp}$	$B_v{}'B_{v\,a}{}^{\div}$		$B_{\perp}{}'B_{\perp}{}^{\times}$
	man	open		door
'The	man	opens	the	door'

	$B_v{}'B_{v\,a}{}^{\div}$		$B_{\perp}{}'B_{\perp}{}^{\times}$
	open		door
'(Someone)	opens	the	door'

	$B_{\perp}{}'B_{\perp}{}^{\times}$	$B_v{}'B_{v\,a}{}^{\div}$
	door	open
'The	door	opens'

Thus it can be seen that semantic features of the verb combined with the deletion or non-deletion of an animate subject cause the choice of the surface subject. This may not only be true for signs but may be a universal feature for languages in general. This is not the same as saying for example that all animate verbs in American Sign Language equate with all animate verbs in every other language. It may be true to a large extent, but that can only be shown through observation and testing. However, the fact that what the speakers of the language consider animate verbs will determine the use or non-use of animate nouns as subjects of these verbs. It will be the job of the linguist to cross-match these features of animateness in verbals and nominals in as many languages as possible.

Fillmore (1968) believes that verbs which involve active participation (Agent) such as 'look' are different from non-active participation (Dative) such as 'see'. This seems to be applicable to English but not to signs. The argument for this relationship in English is based on a surface structure operation for English which shows up in the impossibility of using these dative verbs without agents in imperatives and progressive constructions.

But there is no progressive in American Sign Language and the imperative of 'look' and 'see' are both possible in signs. Therefore, it seems that only the quality of animateness in the verb is the important feature in distinguishing the possibility of inanimate subjects for signs. Other languages perhaps have further modifications on this contrast of animateness.

It is important to note also that verbs may also be marked to account for datives, objects, and objective complements.

$\cap 5_{v\perp}^{\#}$ $B_v/B_v{}_a^{\div}$ $B_\perp/B_\perp^{\times}$
man   open   door
'The   man   opens   the   door'

$K_v K_v{}^{N\sim}$ OF $\cap 5_{v\perp}$ $\cap_v C_v C^{\div}$
people   elect   man   president
'The   people   elect   the   man   president'

$K_v K_v{}^{N\sim}$ $O_T O_{T\perp}^a$ $\cap 5_{v\perp}$ $\cup O_T^{\times}$ ·
people   give   man   food
'The   people   give   the   man   food'

The following rules are necessary to generate the sentences above.

Comment → $\left\{ \begin{array}{l} V \quad OP \\ NP \\ Adj \end{array} \right\}$ (Object Phrase)

$\begin{array}{ccc} V & OP \Rightarrow & V \\ |+object| & & |+object| \end{array}$ $\begin{array}{c} NP \\ |\pm animate| \end{array}$

$\begin{array}{cc} V & OP \Rightarrow \\ \left|\begin{array}{c} +object \\ +dative \end{array}\right| & \end{array}$ $\begin{array}{c} V \\ \left|\begin{array}{c} +object \\ +dative \end{array}\right| \end{array}$ $\begin{array}{c} NP \\ |+animate| \end{array}$ $\begin{array}{c} NP \\ |\pm animate| \end{array}$

$\begin{array}{cc} V & OP \Rightarrow \\ \left|\begin{array}{c} +objective \\ +dative \end{array}\right| & \end{array}$ $\begin{array}{c} V \\ \left|\begin{array}{c} +objective \\ +dative \end{array}\right| \end{array}$ $\begin{array}{c} NP \\ |+animate| \end{array}$ $\begin{array}{c} NP \\ |+animate| \end{array}$

Any of these elements can be deleted later by the deletion rule dealt with below.

To summarize this section, it can be said that although Fillmore's actual case categories may not be accurate for American Sign Language and some other languages, his ideas about the relation of semantics in syntax deserve note. It seems that by attaching features to the verb, case categories may later be generated according to the specific language rules.

Fillmore (1968) feels that the deep structure has no ordering, and only with the specific surface structure does ordering come. Taking his idea one step further, not only is there no ordering in the deep structure, constituents are probably simultaneous. This idea seems logical if we consider that modern semantic and phonological analyses are done by a simultaneous analysis of features. If semantics and phonology have simultaneous parts, why not the syntax, especially in the deep structure?

Sign Language structure can be used as an argument for simultaneous constituents in the deep structure (and surface structure) syntax. Consider the sentences:

(Specific pointing)	he	'He is not eating'
(Shake head)	not	
$\cup O_T^{)(\cdot}$	eat	
$\cup O_T^{)(\cdot}$	eat	'Have you finished eating'
$\phi\,B^{\ddot{o}}$	finish	
(Raise eyebrows)	?	
(Specific pointing)	he	'He is eating'
$\cup O_T^{)(\cdot}$	eat	

Each of these sentences has more than one constituent, yet they are all produced simultaneously. There are various other examples of simultaneousness in American Sign Language, but the real point of the discussion is whether these structures were simultaneous in the deep structure and remained simultaneous in the surface structure, or whether this simultaneousness is only a specific surface feature of American Sign Language.

Lenneberg (1967) seems to provide a possible solution to the proposed problem. He points out that it seems that grammatical structure and physiological capabilities are interrelated. He states (p. 106):

In summary, we see that a sequential chain model fails to account for the facts in more than one way and that a central plan model with hierarchical dominance, ... is more satisfactory. The most interesting implication of this discussion is that formal aspects of purely physiological processes seem to be similar to certain formal aspects of grammatical processes; it appears, in fact, as if the two, physiology and syntax, were intimately related, one grading into the other as it were.

Lashley has pointed out that the problems illustrated by the study of syntax are indeed universal problems of the sequencing of any patterned motor behavior. Thus he foreshadowed a fundamental theme of this book: the foundations of language are ultimately to be found in the physical nature of man — anatomy and physiology — and that language is best regarded as a peculiar adaptation of a very universal physiological process to a species-specific ethological function: communication among members of our species.

Lenneberg's "Plan of the sentence" (Fig. 2) is comparable to the deep structure universals or at least a much deeper than surface structure, and the rest of his diagram is comparable to a derivation from deeper to final surface structures. Ordering comes in because of physical articulatory capabilities in relation to morphemes. However, in signs, physical limitations are less restrictive, and ordering does not have to play an integral role in grammar, although certain orderings (when ordering occurs) are not permitted because of the possibilities of ambiguity.

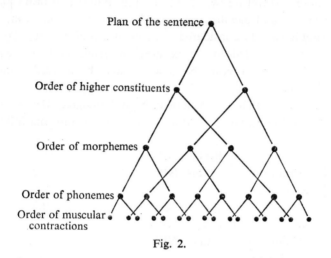

Fig. 2.

Here again, American Sign Language has perhaps given us further insights into the murkiness of deep structure and how specific languages can be related to a universal theory. Deep structure and perhaps a certain part of the thought process is not consecutive, although it would be absurd to assume that some consecutive thought does not occur. But it seems the need and use of consecutiveness is language specific because of articulatory limitations. It should be noted that signs may be simultaneous only in shorter sentences; in longer sentences the order is generally Topic Comment, unless some specific element is chosen to be emphasized.

Postal (1969) has stated that pronouns in English should be considered as special types of articles. It is the writer's belief that not only are pronouns and articles related in American Sign Language, but the process of pronominalization is also related to deletion transformations which act quite frequently in American Sign Language and occasionally in other languages.

As was stated earlier, an attempt should be made to correlate linguistic data with psycho-physical realities in the human individual. One way, perhaps, to gain some psychological insight is to appeal to 'formal' semantic criteria, since in actuality language is a tool for communicating ideas, and it would seem that semantics is more closely related to ideas than syntax is.

Pronominalization is actually a substitution of a closed class of forms for the set of nouns in the language. It seems that to learn something about pronouns, therefore, we should look at nouns and noun phrases. As Chafe (1967) and Jacobs and Rosenbaum (1968) point out, determiners do not have to be considered as a constituent of the deep structure. Actually, it is more fruitful to generate determiners from semantic features in the deep structure NP's which may be derived from even deeper structures.

Now considering that for American Sign Language, the NP's may be marked $\pm$definite and $\pm$proximate, we can generate the following:

$$\begin{vmatrix} \text{NP} \\ +\text{definite} \\ +\text{proximate} \end{vmatrix} \Rightarrow B_a G_v{}^{\times} \text{ NP} \\ \text{'this NP'}$$

$$\begin{vmatrix} \text{NP} \\ +\text{definite} \\ -\text{proximate} \end{vmatrix} \Rightarrow B_a Y_v{}^{\times} \text{ NP} \\ \text{'that NP'}$$

$$\begin{vmatrix} \text{NP} \\ -\text{definite} \end{vmatrix} \Rightarrow \text{NP} \\ \text{'NP'}$$

Deletion transformations take place frequently in some languages, such as Chinese, and less frequently in other languages, such as English, depending on surface structure restrictions. In any deletion process, a Martinet (1964) type of economy is used: what is understood by the speakers is not explicitly stated unless there is a possibility of confusion by listeners. Thus, as was mentioned before, the deep structure possibility of deletion is further delineated by surface grammatical restrictions.

For signs, however, there appear to be no surface structure restrictions on deletion. Therefore a semantic feature of $\pm$understood should be added to the NP constituent, thus generating the following possibilities:

$$\begin{array}{ll}
\text{NP} & \Rightarrow \text{B}_a\text{G}_v{}^{\times} \\
\left|\begin{array}{l}+\text{understood} \\ +\text{definite} \\ +\text{proximate}\end{array}\right| & \text{'this'}
\end{array}$$

$$\begin{array}{ll}
\text{NP} & \Rightarrow \text{B}_a\text{Y}_n{}^{\times} \\
\left|\begin{array}{l}+\text{understood} \\ +\text{definite} \\ -\text{proximate}\end{array}\right| & \text{'that'}
\end{array}$$

$$\begin{array}{ll}
\text{NP} & \Rightarrow \\
\left|\begin{array}{l}+\text{understood} \\ -\text{definite}\end{array}\right| & \phi
\end{array}$$

$$\begin{array}{ll}
\text{NP} & \Rightarrow \text{NP} \\
\left|-\text{understood}\right| & \text{'NP'}
\end{array}$$

The semantic features also have a close relation to the process of pronominalization, as seen from the rules given below.

Pronominalization in signs involves the addition of one more semantic category, $\pm$pronominalization. With $+$pronominalization, the pronoun is generated, with $-$pronominalization, the pronoun is not generated. Note that the pronoun can be generated only when the NP is both $+$understood and $-$definite.

$$\begin{array}{ll}
\text{NP} & \Rightarrow \text{(Specific pointing to person or thing)} \\
\left|\begin{array}{l}+\text{understood} \\ -\text{definite} \\ +\text{pronominalization} \\ +\text{specific}\end{array}\right| &
\end{array}$$

$$\begin{array}{ll}
\text{NP} & \Rightarrow \text{(General pointing away from the} \\
\left|\begin{array}{l}+\text{understood} \\ -\text{definite} \\ +\text{pronominalization}\end{array}\right| & \text{speaker)}
\end{array}$$

$$\begin{array}{ll}
\text{NP} & \Rightarrow \phi \\
\left|\begin{array}{l}+\text{understood} \\ -\text{definite} \\ -\text{pronominalization}\end{array}\right| &
\end{array}$$

From the above analysis, the writer believes that it can be argued that pronominalization, the addition of determiners, and deletion are all basically interrelated semantic processes which may or may not be further limited by surface structures. Furthermore, it might be argued that these semantic processes are universal, but their surface occurrences are limited by the unique grammar of the language in question.

Although embedding has been considered a different process from conjunction by transformationalists such as Chomsky (1957) and Jacobs and Rosenbaum (1968), the writer believes that with American Sign Language, at least, embedding may be viewed as a special surface structure process of conjunction. Transformationalists have handled embedding and conjunction in similar ways, but there seems to have been no explicit comparison made.

Looking at signs, we see the following sentence is possible:

	$\cap 5_{v_{\perp}}^{\#}$			OO_v		$O_v O_{v\perp}^{\eta}$	$\square B_<^{\times}$	XX^{I}
	man			in		store	my	frìend
'The	man	who	is	in	the	store	is	my	friend'

The above sentence is an actual conjoining of two sentences:

	$\cap 5_{v_{\perp}}^{\#}$			OO_v		$O_v O_{v\perp}^{\eta}$
	man			in		store
'The	man	is	in	the	store'

	$\cap 5_{v_{\perp}}^{\#}$		$\square B^{\times}$	XX^{I}
	man		my	friend
'The	man	is	my	friend'

	$\cap 5_{v_{\perp}}^{\#}$			OO_v		$O_v O_{v\perp}^{\eta}$	$\square B^{\times}$	XX^{I}
	man			in		store	my	friend
'The	man	who	is	in	the	store	is	my	friend'

Comparing the above sentences with the following conjunction we find some striking parallels.

	$\cap 5_{v_{\perp}}^{\#}$	$B_a V_v^{z}$
	man	dance
'The	man	danced'

	$\cap 5_{v_{\perp}}^{\#}$	YY^{ω}
	man	play
'The	man	played'

	$\cap 5_{v_{\perp}}^{\#}$	$B_a V_v^{z}$		YY^{ω}
	man	dance		play
'The	man	danced	and	played'

Conjoining is very common in signs, but usually without a conjunction. What actually appeared to be an embedding in the first example seems to be more similar to the actual process of conjunction.

Conjoining in signs is interesting, for it is here we can easily run into surface structure ambiguities, for example:

	$\cap 5_{v\perp}^{\#}$			$B_a 5_v$		$[]B^\times$	$XX^{\mathbb{I}}$
	man			study		my	friend
'The	man	who	is	studying	is	my	friend'

	$\cap 5_{v\perp}^{\#}$		$B_a 5_v$	$[]B^\times$	$XX^{\mathbb{I}}$
	man		study	my	friend
'The	man	is	studying	my	friend'

The differences between these two sentences might be expressed through suprasegmentals (pause, facial expression, etc.) but no definite pattern has been discovered.

Conjoining, combined with deletion rules, can produce sentences that are completely incomprehensible to all but a native signer. For instance:

	$[]\,\overset{\cdots\cdots}{B\,B}{}^\times$				$A'A_T^{>\,\times}$
	have				behind
'I	have	some	money	in	reserve'

This sentence that seems rather strange on the surface has a rather regular development that can be generally outlined as in the tree diagrams below.

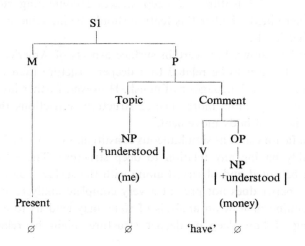

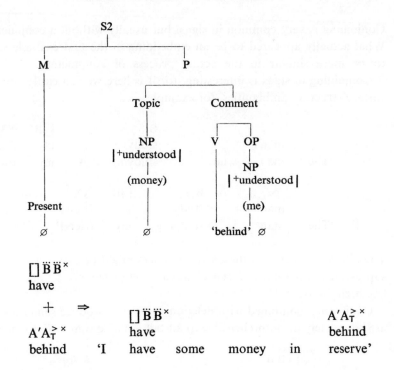

It should be noted that this sentence was used in a situation of an answer to question as to whether the speaker had enough money to buy a new car or not.

Embedding, it seems, can be considered as variant surface phenomena that are not necessarily present as constituent rules in the deep structure, but rather as special features of deep structure conjoining rules. It cannot be determined whether this feature should be introduced on the deep or surface levels.

This paper has shown how certain surface aspects of American Sign Language can be seen to be related to a deeper structure than we find on the surface in such languages as English. However, further investigation into signs may show more surface structure restrictions through facial expression and body movement.

But certain factors such as simultaneous constituents cannot be ignored as not possibly having any relation to deep structure. These 'deeper' factors must be noted and observed along with the surface rules. Thus, although this paper does not present a very complete analysis of signs, it gives an outline of how an analysis of signs may lead us to a better understanding of how deep or deeper structure might be related to actual surface structure occurrences and perhaps give us some insights into the reasons why some languages have developed less surface structure restrictions than others in choosing from the universal deep structure.

The following rules are a recapitulation of the rules previously discussed. It should be noted that these rules actually constitute a small, but integral, part of American Sign Language Grammar. The rules are ordered in the way necessary to produce grammatical sentences.

Deep Structure Rules

$S \rightarrow M\ P$

$M \rightarrow$ Tense, Negation, Question, etc.

$P \rightarrow$ Topic Comment

Topic $\rightarrow$ NP

$$\text{Comment} \rightarrow \begin{Bmatrix} \text{V} & \text{OP} \\ \text{NP} \\ \text{Adj} \end{Bmatrix}$$

Realization Rules

T-1 Sequencing

$$\begin{bmatrix} \text{Topic} \\ \text{Comment} \end{bmatrix} \Rightarrow \text{Topic Comment}$$

where Topic and Comment are too long to be signed simultaneously

T-2 Object Generation-1

$$\begin{array}{ccc} \text{V} & \text{OP} \Rightarrow \text{V} & \text{NP} \\ |+\text{object}| & |+\text{object}| & |\pm\text{animate}| \end{array}$$

T-3 Object Generation-2

$$\begin{array}{cccc} \text{V} & \text{OP} \Rightarrow \text{V} & \text{NP} & \text{NP} \\ \begin{vmatrix} +\text{object} \\ +\text{dative} \end{vmatrix} & \begin{vmatrix} +\text{object} \\ +\text{dative} \end{vmatrix} & |+\text{animate}| & |\pm\text{animate}| \end{array}$$

T-4 Object Generation-3

$$V \qquad OP \Rightarrow V \qquad NP \qquad NP$$

$$\left|\begin{array}{l}+\text{objective}\\+\text{dative}\end{array}\right| \quad \left|\begin{array}{l}+\text{objective}\\+\text{dative}\end{array}\right| \quad \left|+\text{animate}\right| \quad \left|+\text{animate}\right|$$

T-5 Animate Subject

$$NP \qquad V \quad \Rightarrow \quad NP \qquad V$$

$$\left|\propto\text{animate}\right| \quad \left|+\text{animate}\right| \quad \left|\propto\text{animate}\right|$$

T-6 Determiner Generation-1

$$NP \qquad \Rightarrow \qquad NP$$

$$\left|\begin{array}{l}+\text{definite}\\+\text{proximate}\end{array}\right| \qquad \text{'this NP'}$$

T-7 Determiner Generation-2

$$NP \qquad \Rightarrow \qquad NP$$

$$\left|\begin{array}{l}+\text{definite}\\-\text{proximate}\end{array}\right| \qquad \text{'that NP'}$$

T-8 Noun Deletion

$$NP \qquad \Rightarrow \quad \phi$$

$$\left|+\text{understood}\right|$$

Note that T-8 does not delete a generated determiner.

T-9 Pronominalization-1

$$NP \qquad\qquad\qquad \Rightarrow \text{ (Specific pointing to person or thing)}$$

$$\left|\begin{array}{l}+\text{understood}\\-\text{definite}\\+\text{pronominalization}\\+\text{specific}\end{array}\right|$$

T-10 Pronominalization-2

NP   ⇒ (General pointing away from the speaker)

| +understood |
| −definite |
| +pronominalization |
| −specific |

T-11 Inanimate Subject (optional)

V   NP   ⇒   NP   V

| −animate | | −animate | | −animate | | −animate |
| +object | | | | | +object |

REFERENCES, CHAPTER 7

Basova, A. G.,
   1965 *Ocerki po istorii surdopedagogiceski v S.S.S.R.* [Sketches of the History of Deaf Education in the U.S.S.R.] (Moscow, Moskovskij gosudarstvennyj pedagogičeskij institut im. V. I. Lenina).
Best, Harry,
   1943 *Deafness and the Deaf in the United States* (New York, Mac Millan).
Bornstein, Harry, and Barbara Kannapell,
   1969 *New Signs for Instructional Purposes* (= Final report Proj. no. 6-1924, Contr. no. OE 2-6-061924-1890).
Boskis, R. M., and N. G. Morozova,
   1939 "O razvitii mimičeskoj reči gluxogo rebenka i ee roli v processe obučenija i vospitanija gluxonemyx". [On the Development of Signing in the Deaf Child and its Role in the Process of Educating and Training the Deaf and Dumb], *Sbornik Učebno-vospitatel'naja rabota v škole dlja gluxonemyx* 7:10.
Bruner, Jerome,
   1968 *The Achievement of Codes* (= Center for Cognitive Studies, eighth annual report) (Cambridge, Mass., Harvard University Press).
Chafe, Wallace,
   1967 *English Noun Inflection and Related Matters from a Generative Semantic Point of View* (Washington, D.C. CAL/ERIC).
Chomsky, Noam,
   1957 *Syntactic Structures* (The Hague, Mouton).
   1969 "The Current Scene in Linguistics", *Modern Studies in English*, ed. by Reibel and Shane (New York, Prentice-Hall), 3-12.
Cicourel, Aaron V.,
   1968 "L'acquisizione della struttura sociale", *Rassegna Italiana di Sociologia* 9, 211-258.
   1969 *Generative Semantics and the Structure of Social Interaction* (Rome, Luigi Sturzo Institute).
Cicourel, Aaron V., and R. Boese
   1971 "Sign Language Acquisition and the Teaching of Deaf Children", *The Func-*

tions of Language, ed. by Hymes *et al.* (New York, Teachers College Press).
Dolomakan,
1931   "Nužno li izučat' mimiku?" *Žizn' gluxonemyx* 12. [Should one Master Signs?]
Épée, Charles Michel de l',
1776   *L'institution des sourds-muets* (Paris).
1784   *La véritable manière d'instruire les sourds et muets* (Paris) (First published as *L'institution des sourds-muets* [1776]).
Ferguson, Charles A.,
1959   "Diglossia", *Word* 15, 325-340. (Reprinted 1964, *Language in Culture and Society,* ed. by Hymes (New York, Harper and Row).
Fillmore, Charles,
1968   "The Case for Case", *Universals in Linguistic Theory,* ed. by Bach and Harms (New York, Holt).
Fleri, V. I.,
1835   *Gluxonemye, rassmatrivaemye v otnošhenij k ix sostojaniju i k sposobam obrazovanija, samym svojstvennym ix prirode* [The Deaf and Dumb, Considered in Relation to their Status and to the Methods of Education most Proper to their Nature] (St. Petersburg).
Gejl'man, I. F.,
1957   *Ručnaja azbuka i rečevye žesty gluxonemyx* [The Manual Alphabet and Signs of the Deaf and Dumb] (Moscow, Vsesojuznoe Kooperativnoe Izdatel'stvo).
Goldin, Mark,
1968   *Spanish Case and Function* (Washington, D.C. Georgetown University Press).
Gorman, Pierre Patrick,
1960   "Certain Social and Psychological Difficulties Facing the Deaf Person in the English Community", Unpublished Ph.D. Dissertation (Cambridge University).
Greenberg, Joanne,
1970   *In this Sign* (New York, Holt, Rinehart).
Jacobs, Roderick, and Peter Rosenbaum,
1968   *English Transformational Grammar* (Waltham, Mass., Blaisdell).
Kannapell, Barbara, Lillian Hamilton, and Harry Bornstein,
1969   *Signs for Instructional Purposes* (Washington, D.C. Gallaudet College Press).
Kalugina, A.,
1937   "Slovo i žest", [The Word and the Sign], *Žizn' gluxonemyx* 15.
Klima, Edward,
1969   "Relatedness between Grammatical Systems", *Modern Studies in English,* ed. by Reibel and Shane, (New York, Prentice-Hall), 227-246.
Kohl, Herbert R.,
1966   *Language and Education of Deaf Children* (New York, Center for Urban Education).
Krylov, N.,
1936   "Mimika i obščestvennost'" [Signing and the Public], *Žizn' gluxonemyx* 4.
Lenneberg, Eric,
1967   *Biological Foundations of Language* (New York, Wiley).
Mallery, Garrick,
1881   "Sign Language among North American Indians", *First Annual Report of the Bureau of American Ethnology,* ed. by Powell, 263-552.
Marcinovskaja, E. N.,
1964   "Istoričeskij ocerk ispol'zovanija ručnoj azbuki". [Historical Outline of the Use of the Manual Alphabet], *Special'naja škola* 4, 34-38.
1969   "O daktil'noj reči" [On Fingerspelling], *Defektologia* 5, 19-26.

Martinet, André,
   1964   *Elements of General Linguistics* (Chicago, University of Chicago Press).
McCall, Elizabeth A.,
   1965   "A Generative Grammar of Sign", M.A. Thesis (University of Iowa).
McCawley, James,
   1968   "The Role of Semantics in a Grammar", *Universals in Linguistic Theory*,
          ed. by Bach and Harms, (New York, Holt), 125-169.
Mindel, Eugene, and McCay Vernon,
   1971   *They Grow in Silence* (Silver Spring, Md., National Association of the Deaf).
Postal, Paul,
   1969   "On the So-Called 'Pronouns' in English", *Modern Studies in English*, ed.
          by Reibel and Shane (New York, Prentice-Hall).
Schlesinger, I. M.,
   1969   "The Grammar of Sign Language and the Problem of Language Universals"
          (Hebrew University and Israel Institute of Applied Social Research) (Mimeo).
Shunary, Jonathan,
   1969   *Social Background of the Israeli Sign Language* (= *Working Paper* 9, VRA-
          ISR-32-67, DHEW, Social Rehabilitation Service).
Stokoe, William C., Jr.,
   1960   "Sign Language Structure: An Outline of the Visual Communication Systems
          of the American Deaf", *SIL*: O.P.8 (Reissued Washington, D. C., Gallaudet
          College Press).
   1966   "Linguistic Description of Sign Languages", *Georgetown University Mono-
          graph Series* 19, 243-250.
   1970   "Sign Language Diglossia", *SIL* 21.
Stokoe, William C., Jr., Dorothy Casterline, and Carl Croneberg
   1965   *A Dictionary of American Sign Language* (Washington, D. C. Gallaudet
          College Press).
Ziv, Joseph and Tunya
   1964   *Workshop on Interpreting for the Deaf* (Muncie, Ball State Teacher's College)
          [A translation of part of Gejl'man's introduction].
Zykov, S. A.,
   1965   "Mimikozestovaja rec" [The Sign Language], *Pedagogieekaja ènciklopedija*
          2, ed. by I. A. Kairov *et al.* (Moscow, Izdatel'stvo Sovetskaja ènciklopedija),
          831).

8

SIGN LANGUAGE AND BILINGUALISM

A semiotic view of a sign language should include more than its signs, their denotata, and the relation joining them. It should also take in the relation between the semiotic system under scrutiny and others when it is clear that the systems are somehow or other in contact. In the case of American Sign Language the users are usually completely surrounded by and to a large extent participate in the general culture of English-speaking America — with the exception of telephonic communication, music, and other cultural activities not so obviously closed to those who cannot hear. One way to consider the relationship of English and American Sign Language in contact is furnished by the seminal study of Ferguson (1959). (The following is a slightly changed version of an article published in *SIL* [1970]).

Sign Language Diglossia

Ferguson's study of the linguistic and social relationship he calls 'diglossia' adds substantially to understanding of language and social phenomena. His term diglossia for "two or more varieties of the same language ... used by the same speakers under different conditions" fits a number of cases that neither bilingualism nor the use of a single language could explain. As he predicts, "A full explanation of it can be of considerable help in dealing with problems in linguistic description, in historical linguistics, and in language typology". Using Arabic, Modern Greek, Swiss German, and Haitian Creole as defining languages he discovers nine features of diglossia, an explanation that has substantially helped our understanding of these and other languages.

It can help too in dealing with a special problem in linguistics, the use of sign language in communities of deaf persons, more broadly in the whole flourishing sub-culture of deaf Americans. Heretofore there have been several narrow and restrictive views of deaf persons and their language. One view shares all the blindness of ethnocentricity. It holds that there is but one language, that of the holder, of course, which must also be the language of all deaf persons within the sound of that language. A counter view holds that the language of signs is the language of the deaf community and must be promoted at all costs. A view more recent is that the deaf community is perforce, and the deaf individual more or less, bilingual in the language of the total culture and in sign language. Resolution of these differences in view has been hindered by a number of special interests and naturally by the fact that one of these languages operates in the normal way with vocal symbols while the other uses visual symbols.

Leaving aside for the moment the serious questions of epistemology and linguistic theory these differences pose, I would like to use Ferguson's nine features of diglossia to examine the two varieties of sign language used by deaf persons in America.

At the outset it must be understood that some dimensions of the problem are changed. When the language under study is sign language, the H ('superposed' or 'high') variety is English. However this is English in a form most unfamiliar to usual linguistic scrutiny. It is not spoken but uttered in 'words' which are fingerspelled or signed. The name for this in H is 'The Language of Signs' or 'correct signing' or 'straight language'. Since linguistic study of sign language has increased awareness of the L variety, several have suggested the name 'Manual English' for H. The names for L, the ordinary conversational language, differ too. In H it is called simply 'signs' or 'signing', the sign made is the one which translates these English words. Or it may be called 'conversation' using the sign $\phi \sqrt{G} \sqrt{G^z}$. However this sign may also be used for H or spoken English. In L, the names for L are signs glossed 'talk' or 'chat'. These signs and their distribution are discussed on four pages in Stokoe (1965: 159-162), an instance of where diglossia could have helped to sort an intricate formal and semantic tangle.

(1) Ferguson's table, showing 'the specialization of function for H and L', is reproduced in Fig. 21 with the symbols 's' for sign language H and L added, and the symbol 'o' for cases where the distinction does not apply.

	H	L
Sermon in church or mosque	× s	
Instructions to servants, waiters, workmen, clerks		× s
Personal letters	× sᵃ	
Speech in parliament, political speech	× s	
University lecture	× s	
Conversation with family, friends, colleagues		× s
News broadcast	× o	
Radio 'soap opera'		× o
Newspaper editorial, news story caption on news picture	× sᵃ	
Caption on political cartoonᵇ		× s
Poetryᶜ	× s	
Folk literature		× s

ᵃ Sign language H is written of course in standard English orthography and read likewise.
ᵇ Student posters and papers may use L glossed in 'slang' for captioning cartoons.
ᶜ Poetry and songs recited in H, with rhythm and grace of movement cultivated, are favored entertainment and serve as binders of the community and bridges to 'hearing' culture. Folk literature and humorous skits are always in L and are 'inside' activities; while full dress dramatic performances used to be in H and were shown with pride to outsiders.

Fig. 21.

(2) About the second feature, prestige, Ferguson says: "In all the defining languages the speakers regard H as superior to L in a number of respects. Sometimes the feeling is so strong that H alone is regarded as real and L is reported 'not to exist'." The writer setting out to study 'sign language' in 1957 (the year before Ferguson's first version was read to the American Anthropological Association) encountered only signers who used H and denied any real knowledge of L. One admitted that he "might sign a little differently" to his wife and children than he signed at college. But most of them were seen using signs and ordering them in a way now called L, when they were not talking to the writer about sign language. Non-deaf recruits to the Gallaudet College faculty are now taught sign language formally, but for years newcomers would ask help of deaf colleagues. In both situations it is H that is taught. Ferguson: "If a non-speaker of Arabic asks an educated Arab for help in learning to speak Arabic the Arab will normally try to teach him H forms, insisting that these are the only ones to use".

Educated users of sign language sometimes refer to 'those deaf' and their 'awful signing', meaning uneducated persons and L variety of sign language, but forgetful or unaware that they too use L for the situations indicated in the table. To them of course it is too evident to need stating that English is superior, "more beautiful, more logical, better able to express important thoughts ..." However here the peculiar nature of sign language diglossia appears. When educational power structures or state legislatures prohibit sign language, the educated signers plead for 'our beautiful (or beloved) sign language' meaning H. These cogent and eloquent pleas may be found as early as 1847 in the *American Annals of the Deaf* and as recently as today in *The Deaf American* and publications of regional or state associations of the deaf. That is, in one set of circumstances H is considered simply 'English'; in another it is considered 'sign language' by the same persons. Moreover the sign language community includes bilinguals, hearing speakers of English and users of sign language too. But such are the tensions of sign language diglossia that some of these become the most vehement deniers of the existence of L while others move freely between H and L and spoken English and become most valuable interpreters not just of language but of those aspects of hearing culture not directly accessible to the deaf. There is unfortunately almost no cultural interpretation in the reverse direction.

In spite of these interpreters, always in scarce supply, such is the prestige of H (or English), that many educated signers accept, or are made uneasy by, the repeated statements that sign language is no language at all, has no grammar, is but a collection of "gestures ... suggestive of ... ideas" See p. 57 above — it would be invidious as well as incriminating to cite all the sources of these much plagiarized non-statements about American Sign Language. Makers of such secondary and tertiary responses to sign language range from bilinguals who themselves use L with great effect on occasion to outsiders who make it a point of pride not to learn one form of H or L. Certainly the linguistic schizophrenia they induce is one problem the explanation offered by Ferguson can help cure.

In the matter of literary heritage, sign language H can claim all the literature written in English, for written English is as accessible to the educated signer as to the native speaker — given equal educational opportunities. But again the signer faces a dichotomy in addition to diglossia. When he reads 'aloud' from a literary work, he is using H, but his formal education may have taught him, out of awareness, to feel that just as H is superior to L, so spoken and heard English is superior to signed. 'One man's H another man's L' is too true to be funny, and the tensions of a normal diglossia are intensified. This over and above the kind of teaching that convinces a speaker of dialect that Shakespeare, Wordsworth, and Henry James belong forever only to his teachers and other speakers of standard, if he has not already dropped out before they appear in his education.

(3) In the method of acquisition too, sign language diglossia differs from that of Ferguson's four defining languages, but in a way that seems to confirm his general principles. Deaf adults use L in signing to their deaf or hard of hearing children, and deaf children sign to one another in L. But educated deaf adults make a conscious effort to use and teach H (English). Thus the only children that learn L in the 'normal' way are those whose family linguistic environment is sign language or bilingual (spoken English and sign language), a small minority.

Others learn L from other children earlier or later as they come together in schools and more or less 'normally' as the schools permit or prohibit signing. Signers may not remember when they first used signs (L) or may 'never' have used them until leaving school and finding their way into deaf groups. Of course different signers' ease in the language differs greatly not only for these reasons but also because human beings who cannot hear use and develop incipiently linguistic visual symbol systems which interfere with L in various ways. The 'native' speaker of L often speaks of those come to it lately as using 'home-signs' (this is the L term; they are called 'home-made signs' in H).

For the signer, even learning H is not like the typical case of learning H in diglossia. Schools that are permissive 'teach English' and undertake no formal instruction in H, signed English. However, the best teachers, often themselves deaf, regularly use H AND L in teaching the Three R's and the rest of the curriculum — separating H and L exactly as do teachers in the defining languages.

Another of Ferguson's observations about language acquisition is so pertinent here it deserves quotation in full after an emphatic condition: EVEN SHOULD HE LEARN SIGN LANGUAGE LATE IN LIFE, "The speaker is at home in L to a degree he almost never achieves in H. The grammatical structure of L is learned without explicit discussion of grammatical concepts; the grammar of H is learned in terms of 'rules' and norms to be imitated".

(4) Unlike Arabs who want H to replace L completely, signers do not propose to make everyone use H, because they are too realistic to expect all English speakers to use H, convenient as that would be to the sign language community. Nevertheless there are educational specialists who advocate the 'Rochester Method'. This is an artificial H, if one may augment the terminology of diglossia. Using it the child and all around him fingerspell every word; signs are forbidden. Thus the utterance spelled is not normal spoken English but written English —

or what would be written if graphic symbols were used instead of dactylo-logical. Stating the claims for it in the terms of diglossia mingled with the terms of its advocates: children would acquire good H in the 'normal' way, ungrammatical L would disappear, and the barbarous and destruct-ive interference of L with H would cease. But of course diglossia gives no evidence that there is interference.

The most important fact of language acquisition by the deaf child, seen from the viewpoint afforded by examining diglossia, is that the English (oral, written, or H) which he acquires is the English that has been presented to him in explicit discussion, formal education. There is not only "a strong tradition of the grammatical study of the H form" but there are also special grammars, methods, and aids for teaching it to children who cannot hear. Épée's and Siccard's methodical signs, Wing's Symbols, The Fitzgerald Key, The Barry Five Slates, The Northampton Charts — methods spanning two hundred years are added to the libraries of English grammars, dictionaries, and style manuals. This of course accounts only for the English component of H. There are also handbooks, manuals, and vade-mecums telling and showing usually the non-user of L how the forms of H should be properly made. Until 1960 not one took any more notice of L than to mention in passing that sometimes 'slang' or 'unacceptable' signs might be seen but should be avoided. In 1965 Stokoe, Croneberg, and Casterline in the *Dictionary of American Sign Language* attempted to describe both H and L (though without knowing and using Ferguson's clear insight or terminology). A number of additional normative sign handbooks have appeared since.

(5) Toward standardization signers take an interesting stance. Mem-bers of the sign community regularly commend the writer for his lin-guistic studies as if, or ask if, his purpose is to 'standardize the sign language'. It is felt that to do so would be a good thing; but in this context one may suppose that the vague though deep feeling is a desire (1) to reduce the differences between the regional L's, (2) to corroborate the position of some center like Gallaudet College to have the standard L, (3) to label clearly H forms and L forms as such, and even in some, (4) to exclude the L forms from good company.

(6) In stability and persistence sign language diglossia appears typical. Educated deaf persons were numerous enough to make a linguistic community with some political thrust in Paris education before the end of the Napoleonic era. The differences between Épée's *signes méthodi-ques* and what he calls *signes naturelles* are described by Épée himself and other writers in terms that clearly identify them as H and L respect-

ively. More scattered allusions to different 'varieties' or 'correctness' of signing in The United States points to a H and L from 1817. But this crossing of the Atlantic may not immediately have transformed H and L into English and conversational signs. There is considerable evidence for thinking that for some time after 1817 H in the American signing community was in some respects closer to French than to English (there is also a great need for more historical study of sign language). At least early writers attest to the placement of substantive first in two-sign phrases, but teachers of H as late as 1955 were maintaining that adjective sign following noun sign was 'correct' — a notion youngsters raised in L soon dispelled.

(7) On the score of grammar, sign language might have been one of the languages Ferguson used for defining diglossia: "One of the most striking differences ... is in the grammatical structure: H has grammatical categories not present in L and has an inflectional system of nouns and verbs which is much reduced or totally absent in L." "Also, in every one of the defining languages there seem to be several striking differences of word order as well as a thorough-going set of differences in the use of introductory and connective particles ... THERE ARE ALWAYS EXTENSIVE DIFFERENCES BETWEEN THE GRAMMATICAL STRUCTURES OF H AND L." (The emphasis is Ferguson's).

It is possible to say that H in sign language has all the inflectional systems of English. So it does potentially, and actually when a word is spelled, not signed. Indeed the H sign-morpheme 'apostrophe s' (ϕ A$_s{}^a$) or 's apostrophe' can make visible a distinction not expressed in English speech. But even a signed noun in H may have a plural suffix. Some signers repeat the SIG (minimally contrastive movement) of a noun sign for plural. But in L, nouns are uninflected. L verbs are likewise uninflected.

Sign language L is 'simpler' in grammar according to the four tests Ferguson gives. It shows greater difference from H than is shown by any of the four defining languages, when H is equivalent to manually presented English.

(a) Thus L has no morpheme alternants in its grammatical system, since its signs remain uninflected.

(b) It is without obligatory categories and has no need to observe concord.

(c) Paradigms are simpler to the point of non-existence.

(d) And since inflection is not found, rection could not be simpler. Adjuncts in L for example are all compared by placing the sign 'more' or 'most' before them. Moreover H uses the articles of English, finger-spelling them because L has none. The same is true of the copula, non-existent in L.

(8) Regarding vocabulary it can be said of sign language as of the defining languages, that "the bulk of the vocabulary of H and L is shared". Although the *Dictionary* lists only some 3,000 signs, these are for the most part signs that can serve both H and L, and also they are more than sufficient for L users in the functions L serves. Conversely, as Ferguson adds, H has "technical terms and learned expressions which have no regular L equivalents, since the subjects involved are rarely if ever discussed in pure L". This accounts for the whole technical and learned vocabulary of English which is in H both through fingerspelling and through the nonce coinage of signs in special situations, some of which remain as items in the H vocabulary (see Chapter 7).

Sign language diglossia also is typical in that L has borrowed a number of H terms, while the prestige of H serves to keep L signs out. Uncounted times in checking dictionary entries with educated signers the compilers would be told: "That sign is all right for ordinary conversation, but ..." It might be thought that this one-way gating between H and L and the relatively small L vocabulary would prevent users of L from operating effectively — is L a 'primitive' language? The fact is that such subjects as mathematical concepts, poetic theory, and principles of historiography are of course presented in H; but they may be understood in L. That is, the translation of such matters from the special vocabulary and intricate grammar of H into the signs and context free grammar of L may be most illuminating — "tell me in words of one syllable" — for both deaf and hearing users of sign language.

Another "striking feature of diglossia is the existence of many paired items, one H one L ..." It is obvious on first look that a signer is using H not L when he fingerspells short words that have signs in L. *At, on, in* — all the prepositions signed in L are spelled in H. One reason is that L signs that gloss English prepositions are not regularly the prepo-sitions' equivalents in many of their uses. Another is that in H the object of a preposition may have to be fingerspelled. Using two letters of the manual alphabet may be 'easier' as teachers of H say; but equally, moving the spelling hand away from spelling position to make the L preposition and back will make the spelling harder to read. Put posi-tively, spelling the preposition alerts the reader to watch for spelled item coming. Pairs, spelled in H, signed in L, are not limited to prepositions. Conjunctions present a number of variations on the typical pairing of diglossia. The sign 'and' is shared. That is teachers of H and manuals note that this sign is the only sign permitted in fingerspelling. (Recall that typically H is taught formally, prescriptively). The sign 'but' is often used in H signing where it makes a sharper rhetorical break than the spelled word can do; and in fact it makes an excellent reinforcing, rhetorical gesture even completely outside the sign language community. The 'or' is more a part of L, perhaps because as with prepositions vocabulary used contiguously in H may require fingerspelling.

But even nouns and verbs show H and L pairing. *Hat, cat, food, eat, sit, go,* and many more are regularly fingerspelled in H though they may be signed, but always signed in L. Another place to look for H and L pairs is in the vocabulary of institutional life: refectory, dormitory, recreation have their L vocabulary which is translatable to be sure into English words, but which H perhaps is felt too grand to acknowledge. More investigation is needed to make a complete statement about H and L vocabulary. Doubtless many of the *Dictionary* classifications will be clarified and the whole vexed question of usage or style levels more sensibly answered when ASL can be thoroughly studied with diglossia as a guide.

There is a 'question-sign' in H, the index finger crooking and straightening draws a question mark about two inches high. L does not use this sign but substitutes for normal clause terminal a question terminal. Also H has a sign for 'apostrophe s'. Although it is used at the end of a fingerspelled noun it will also make a possessive when it follows a personal-name or noun sign, L does not use this sign but uses the flat hand, palm toward the possessor, a sign that is more like a possessive pronoun than like a morpheme to be added to names or nouns.

(9) Like any consideration of phonology, Ferguson's crucial statements about the phonology of H and L in diglossia need adjustment to a language that uses visual elements in place of sounds. Here is the first: "1. The sound systems of H and L constitute a single phonological structure of which the L phonology is the basic system and the divergent features of H phonology are either a subsystem or a parasystem".

Do H and L constitute a single GESTEMIC[1] system? Mallery (1881) develops at length a theory that there is but one gestemic system common not only to the world's sign language users but to all human creatures. Studies in semiotics support his view, emphasizing the functional identify in animal communication as divergent as silkworm scents, wolf howls,

---

[1] This term (Kakamasu, 1968; Ljung, 1965) makes an excellent paralabel to PHONOLOGICAL, leaving the writer's CHEREMIC approximately equivalent to PHONEMIC.

and gorilla gestures (Sebeok, 1969). Cultural anthropology seems to run counter to Mallery, paying particular attention to the differences between, and the internal consistency of, culture-bound human systems.

Perhaps sign language linguistics can resolve the apparent contradiction. There is certainly a prelinguistic phonetics — mynah birds, many mammals, and black boxes in acoustics laboratories share with man the capacity for making sounds that are enough alike to be mistaken for each other. However once the context is a particular language instead of similar sounds, phonology of that language takes on a more restrictive meaning. One can speak too of pre-linguistic gestemics. And there is no reason why this cannot be widely enough defined to include bee or cock grouse dancing, chimpanzee grimacing, human kinesics (a parasystem to language: Birdwhistell, 1952), and sign languages. Again once the universe of discourse is narrowed to a particular sign language, the gestemic inventory of that language and its cheremes, its minimal contrasting symbols, become the issue. That other folk in another time or place also move the hand to the mouth to signify 'eat' is now irrelevant.

Of course this does not contradict Mallery. Since all peoples and some of the animal kingdom use gestemics, encountering those who use gestemic symbols organized in a more or less completely linguistic way does not seem strange. However before his projection of 'universal sign language' can be realized, it will be necessary for general pre-linguistic gestemics to be developed the world over into a single system of cheremics, morphology, and semology.

According to a paraphrase then of Ferguson's statement above: the gestemics of H and L constitute a single gestemic structure of which the L gestemics is the basic system and the divergent features of H gestemics are either a subsystem or a parasystem. This is so true of American Sign Language that until the appearance of Ferguson's explanation of diglossia the existence of the two varieties side by side remained unsuspected. Much of the contradiction, controversy, and patent nonsense in published statements about ASL stems form a situation much like that in *The Comedy of Errors* and its Roman and Greek sources. How can Gremio deny he received the money five minutes before? Quite honestly; that was Grumio. How can a beautiful, articulate, nuance-filled language be completely without grammar? Simply when H and L are not distinguished — and with the further stipulation that the non-linguists who charge that sign language has no grammar must be understood to be saying only that it has none of the inflectional features of English.

The gestemic structure of L serves H as well, but even the non-signing observer will be struck with the different ways different signers in different circumstances make 'the same sign'. Many factors account for this. Regional dialects (Croneberg, 1965), men's and women's sign language, age of signers (Stokoe, 1965), and style level and situation. This last, though, has been given some precise bearings by Ferguson's account.

In using H the signer 'refines' his L gestemics. Body parts that were approached in L may be touched noticeably. Hands that were held loosely are tightened into more precise configurations. Movements that flow from one sign to another (sandhi) are omitted and each sign is made with almost military precision. This is the extreme range of H-L contrast, the difference say between a deaf lay-preacher making an invocation in chapel and discussing a volleyball game in the locker-room. But even where the difference is this great, what has been described is no more than the substitution of one allocher for another. The cheremic system embraces them both.

Fingerspelling may be counted a divergent feature of H gestemics. A hand (configuration-presentation) symbolizes an alphabetic symbol and is non cheremic in the context of other such c-p's. A DEZ, i.e. a cheremic configuration (which may look identical with an alphabetic c-p), works with a cheremic place, TAB, to make a cheremic action, SIG. A dez stays the same dez though it may turn over or back to front in making a sig. But the same configuration in fingerspelling is 'u' presented pointing up, is 'n' pointing down, and is 'h' pointing to the side. The index finger held horizontal is 'g', downward is 'q'. Fingerspelling requires signer and reader to distinguish these differences as well as configurations such as 's', 't', and 'a', which are similar enough to be allochers of one L chereme. Thus fingerspelling is a subsystem of sign language.

Looking at the gestemic structure from morphemics, one sees the elements of L and H morphemes as cheremes but also sees that finger-spelling is a parasystem. Its elements form the words of H just as letters from the words of written English. Semologically too, fingerspelling is a parasystem. H and L dez cheremes have little or no meaning apart from the tab and sig cheremes associated with them in signs, but a configura-tion-presentation of fingerspelling 'means' letters of English orthography.

Again, a characteristic of diglossia according to Ferguson: "2. If 'pure' H items have phonemes not found in 'pure' L items, L phonemes frequently substitute for these in oral use of H ..." In sign language H, dez cheremes for INITIAL-DEZ signs retain their strict fingerspelling configuration, but when these signs are used in L, the configuration becomes a chereme of L. For example there is very little difference between the 'k' and 'v' c-p's of fingerspelling. In the former the thumb tip rests on the middle joint of the middle finger. In the latter it is against the folded-in ring finger. Nevertheless signs like 'keep' and 'supervise' in H preserve this distinction which may be taken to establish 'K' and 'V' as cheremes in H. These signs in L are likely to show no difference in configuration, reducing the two cheremes to one.

The foregoing statements about sign language diglossia are incomplete and subject to revision as more study of sign language verifies, modifies, or discredits them. Nevertheless, taking the position that diglossia is the situation can certainly be "of considerable help in dealing with problems in linguistic description", as should be clear. Another advantage of examining both H and L is the guidance it can provide in dealing with questions of language policy. Knowledge that sign language embraces not only L but also H, which has morphological and semological identity with English, is preferable to uninformed opinion that sign language is agrammatical and hampers its users' mental development. Knowledge that diglossia is "a relatively stable language situation" today and in the past should reduce the amount of energy and resources wasted in trying to turn sign language L into 'pure' H (Quigley, 1968), in trying to prevent L from corrupting H, and in trying to extirpate both (Fabray, 1968).

Before the sociolinguistic concomitants of sign language diglossia are further explored it is necessary to recall how special a situation it is. Ferguson points out that, "Diglossia seems to be accepted and not regarded as a 'problem' by the community in which it is in force, until certain trends appear in the community. These include trends toward (1) more widespread literacy ... (2) broader communication among different regional and social segments of the community ... (3) desire for a full-fledged 'national' language as an attribute of autonomy or sovereignty."

First it is chiefly to those concerned with the education of the deaf but outside the linguistic community that sign language and diglossia present a 'problem'. Their concern, well intentioned as it may be, can create serious problems for the community when it takes the form of statutes against the use of sign language in schools or of educational policy which effectively keeps signs underground for the first three or four years — thus delaying the time when the user of L learns H and moves from a childish L to that of the community. This educational pressure from without forestalls the trend toward more widespread literacy. The educated and uneducated adult members of the community want all their children who cannot hear to be literate and as highly educated as possible IN H, which is English gestemically instead of phonemically uttered and understood. But their children who cannot hear are a minority. Most are not born into the community but join it at schools or perhaps not until four or five years after leaving school (Gorman, 1960). Most of the parents of children who cannot hear are not themselves members and many may actively wish their children not to become members of the linguistic community under discussion. But this does not solve the problems.

Second the desire for broader communication within the community has posed a minor problem for the writer. English-Sign Manuals, and classes in sign language (H of course), have proliferated while within the community reaction to the *Dictionary* (1965) in which both L and H items were included has been similar to that aroused by a new un-abridged dictionary of English. It is only fair to say that more of the reaction has been favorable. But hopes expressed that the *Dictionary* would 'standardize' the language reflect the unease diglossia can generate. The great need of course is for a Dante of sign language who can convince the community that the vernacular has life that is denied to the H variety as he enriches the world with creation in L.

Although the parallels are often very close between sign language H and L and the two varieties of the defining languages Ferguson used, diglossia is not necessarily the language situation of every user of American Sign Language. Those signers who received very little formal education in English or whose experiences with it have been non-productive may have so limited a knowledge of sign language H as to be virtually monolingual. They may however exhibit typical attitudes toward L and H. An entirely different departure from the diglossia defined above is taken by a small number of deaf persons who are becoming aware of the new interest of linguists and sociolinguists in bilingualism and bilingual education. In the case of American Sign Language/American English users who cannot hear, the difference between diglossia and bilingualism is a difference in degree or emphasis. Instead of thinking of sign language in terms of H and L varieties, they face the major differences in the systems and speak of two separate languages, English and 'idiomatic' sign language. There are virtues in both attitudes toward this special language duality.

A better grasp of the latter attitude and some insight into language acquisition will come from reading the following section, written by a student in the writer's course in applied linguistics, and recently entered in the ERIC document reproduction system at the Center for Applied Linguistics (Educational Resources Information Center, Clearinghouse in Linguistics and Uncommonly Taught Foreign Languages).

BILINGUAL EXPERIENCES OF A DEAF CHILD (WILLIAMS, 1968)

My husband and I had long expected that our children would have impaired hearing. Our genetic makeup showed this: our parents, my uncle and his four sons are deaf on my side, and four uncles on his side. And so are we. I was born deaf. My husband lost his hearing at the age of six months during an attack of whooping cough, which could be a sign that he was easily susceptible to deafness. When our son Todd was born, he showed so much alertness with his eyes and was so unresponsive to normal sounds that we knew he was like us.

My main concern was not his inability to hear (he is nearly five now and I still don't even give it a thought), but was instead how well he could live within the hearing world. His language acquisition was far more important, since this could open many channels for him including speech, lipreading, manual communication, and writing. The most important part was being able at an early age to express himself linguistically in the simplest forms. Lack of this ability can lead to personality and psychological problems. So I started talking to him like all mothers do, cooing, babbling, singing nursery rhymes and the like — but I added signs and fingerspelling while doing all this.

It was not until he was nine months old that he finally expressed himself clearly in sign language. He loved to throw his spoon on the floor from his high chair and yell for me to pick it up. I always asked him, signing and speaking, 'Where is the spoon?' pointing to it before picking it up. This time he threw it again but asked me in signs, '*Where spoon?*' and pointed at it. This led soon to his substituting in this frame other signs (words) like *ball, light, cat, dog,* and *book*; and we went on to using the 'Pictionary' and 'First Objects' and other books I read to him from while he looked at the objects pictured. By the time he was one year old he was able to identify about fifteen different things in short sentences. His vocabulary increased, but it was not until after he was toilet trained (at about twenty months) that I introduced him to fingerspelling and put a lot of stress on this way of presenting words. He mastered this kind of communication of sentences on his level in a few months and he associated the manual alphabet with the written alphabet. At twenty-five months he started reading, and when he was turning three he had five hundred words in his reading vocabulary and loved to read pre-primers and beginning-to-read books. His language developed in the simultaneous sense, that is, through lipreading my speech, fingerspelling printed matter, and signs. I see no conflict in his bilingual acquisition of English and Sign Language but believe that it greatly aided him. He loved nursery rhymes and was able to recite them himself. He eventually used his speech and sang some syllables out loud.

I enrolled him in the Gallaudet College preschool when he was thirty months old, and its program gave him a lot of auditory training and speech work which I was not able to give him at home. His hearing aid did wonders (although he has an 85 decibel loss in both ears across the whole frequency range), and he responded more to speech and showed willingness to learn to say words accurately.

From this point everything else seemed to come naturally, and his curiosity brought him even further, until I would say that he is progressing just as normally as hearing children do except that he is less vocal. He learned spoken English very readily in expressive exercises, routines, monologues, and interpretations as well as in social responses and requests for information as the situation required. Simplification of grammatical structures was necessary in the early stages, but now at four years and ten months he simplifies them himself for his sister Tiffany two years younger and elaborates the patterns for his Daddy.

His bilingual experience is in some ways like and in others unlike that of the American-Japanese bilinguals studied by Susan Erwin-Tripp (1964). Todd has a more general knowledge of American Sign Language because that is the language more often used at home, and a specific knowledge of English from his education at home and in school. His is really a merger of the two languages therefore, as in the case of the Japanese women who tend to use Japanese for social intercourse and as their base language when with other bilinguals but who do use English as the situation and the persons talked to require. Todd relies more on his signs than on his English with his family and more on spoken English in the classroom.

As Erwin-Tripp says, "... bilinguals who speak only with other bilinguals may be on the road to merger of the two languages, unless there are strong pressures to insulate by topic or setting". Her hypothesis is that "as language shifts, content will shift". And she presents examples of the Japanese women's monologues in which *moon, moon-viewing, zebra-grass, full moon* and *cloud* are in Japanese and *sky rocket* and *cloud* are in English. This kind of difference needs more study in the case of Sign Language-English bilinguals. There may even be a trilingual situation — some words in signs, some spoken, and some English spelled in the manual alphabet depending on the who, where, and what of the communication.

Another observation of hers is that the Japanese women "were in an abnormal situation" when one was asked to speak English with another Japanese woman. The effects on the style of English were clear when the two situations were compared. With the Japanese listener there was much more disruption of English syntax, more intrusion of Japanese words, and briefer speech.

This is also true in cases where two deaf children are forced to speak English to each other. I notice that Todd in this situation shortens his statements and tries to add signs between them. He uses more complex ideas, structures, and words in signs than in spoken English.

In school his English is more or less that of a four-year old in a pre-school situation. But at home when he was three years old, he asked me at the table (in signs) "Where does the meat go?" I asked him what he meant, and he replied: "Look, I swallow the meat, and where does it go?" I then explained to him in details he could understand and he was pleased and satisfied with the answer. Another time, about six months later, he asked me where a sound he was listening to came from. I told him I didn't know, but he insisted that I listen. I had to clarify my position by telling him that I couldn't hear anything at all but that he, Tiffany and Daddy have a little hearing. He was very much hurt by this and offered me his hearing aid, hoping I would respond to sound. When he learned that it was of no help, he cried and was upset for a while. Later I told him he could help me by telling me to move the car over when he hears fire engines or ambulances passing by, because I must give them the right of way. He now delights in telling me when he hears a siren, and he lets me know when he hears a sound and identifies it for me: the vacuum cleaner, someone knocking on the door, and the like. He doesn't have much hearing but uses his residual hearing well and intelligently.

Are there any deaf children his age without sign language who can express themselves this well, ask such questions, and make such distinctions? There are none that I know of. Knowing signs also helps Todd in learning English vocabulary. For example, Todd learned about a zebra in school but not the sign for it. When he came home he told me about the characteristics of this new animal so I could easily identify what he was trying to find out — both of us using his 'base' language of signs.

For young deaf children the most important contribution of sign language is to the child's expression of his needs, questions, and responses. With it he can also develop other channels of language and expression. Without it he may have some receptive competence, if he happens to be a very good lipreader, but he will be terribly hampered in his formative preschool years. Moreover the spoken language the teachers are trying to instill in him becomes warped because he can't really use it expressively to ask questions and to make and try out corrections after being told of his grammatical mistakes.

Sign language has advantages for the hearing children of deaf parents as well. Their bilingual experience of serving their parents by making phone calls and receiving spoken messages can be very valuable. As they use both languages they translate from one to the other. The need to interpret for deaf parents makes them listen to adult conversation with more than normal childish attention. In return they get top grades in reading, spelling, grammar, and other subjects in school, as I found when I made a personal survey of my parents' deaf friends who have hearing children, about forty in all.

These observations agree with the results of Kathryn Meadow's study (1968). She notes that many professionals warn parents against sign language in case children are motivated not to learn speechreading and speech. Her study proves these fears false and shows that deaf children that are exposed to sign language in early childhood have better reading, speechreading, and written language scores. She concludes that "the deaf children of deaf parents [who use sign language] have a higher level of intellectual functioning, social functioning, maturity, independence, communicative competence in written, spoken, expressive, and receptive language".

Sign language is not incompatible with English. In fact with some care about its order and by spelling English function words it can be made into a visual equivalent of English utterance. Unfortunately there is not a school in the United States that uses it as a medium of communication between teacher and pupil except in the advanced department. That is too late.

The experiences of Mrs. Williams and of several other graduate teachers in training who are also students in the writer's course in sign language grammar confirm the observation in the paper just quoted. They have worked with pupils who can, when requested to, shift from sign language sentences, e.g. 'Water I go please?' to signed ('straight') English, e.g. 'Please may I get some water?' But this ability to shift codes belongs only to those pupils who have a genuine competence in sign language to operate from. Pupils who are still signing at the level of 'pivot and open class' structures (McNeill, 1966) have too little competence for translation into a language where their competence is nil.

Assessment of pupils' language competence is a subjective judgment still, but these observers are experienced and they are linguistically sophisticated. When a ten-year-old in a special class (until recently pupils in the class had been judged mentally defective or brain damaged) produces the signs 'dirty' and 'Simon' in that order, the observer sees a close analogue of a sentence like *pretty shoe* in Braine's data (McNeill, 1966: 22). The sign 'dirty' seems to be a pivot, and 'Simon' which another name may replace is clearly open-class. However, in another class, when an alert, energetic, twelve-year-old who engages in long animated complex sign conversations signs 'cheat push', the student-teacher observing sees a very different structure.

Suppose the first rule in ASL grammar is to rewrite Sentence as Topic and Comment or as Comment and Topic (see Chapter 7); then the second rule might be double, recursive, and an optional transformation: rewrite Topic or Comment as Sentence. Exploration of the full structure of 'cheat push' soon shows that 'you cheated' and 'you pushed' are generated. The presence of 'you' is apparent to any observer who takes in the facial communicative activity of the signer (see Ch. 6). Even though it is clear that two sentences, 'you cheated' and 'you pushed' are to be dealt with, it is not possible to characterize the resulting two-sign sentence as either SV SV or as SV SV in surface structure. Nor is SV SV a possible symbolization: the (facial) sign 'you' is present while both verb signs 'push' and 'cheat' are made.

A possible analysis shows both sentences related as topic and comment as in Fig. 22. Some confirmation of this tentative analysis is offered by a longer sign sentence observed in the same class, i.e. among pupils with sign language competence. The sentence in signs is 'I basketball win nothing'. The observer had been following the whole situation in which this sentence occurred. It is not a negative, far from it. The boy was saying, 'I won in basket shooting; nothing to it'. The sign 'nothing' then is a comment on the whole previous structure, and the analysis may be that shown in Fig. 23.

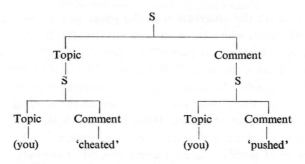

English: *You cheated by pushing.*

Fig. 22.

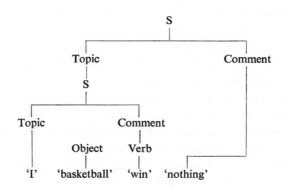

English: *I won in basket-shooting; no bother.*

Fig. 23.

These last two sentences are thus given structural analyses quite different from that of 'dirty' 'Simon', which is simply comment followed by topic. All this analysis depends heavily on the intuition of the observers; however, it should be noted that the observers are themselves native signers, that they recorded all the circumstances in which these sentences and many like them were produced, that they have a keen eye for participant situations, that they 'read' the signers producing the sentences very well, and that with their interest in linguistic problems and solutions it is likely that they will be able in time to make more explicit their grammars of sign language.

REFERENCES, CHAPTER 8

The American Annals of the Deaf,
1847
Barry, K. E.,
1899   *The Five Slate System* (Philadelphia).
Birdwhistell, Ray L.,
1952   *Introduction to Kinesics* (Washington, D.C., Foreign Service Institute).
Croneberg, Carl G.,
1965   "Sign Language Dialects", *A Dictionary of American Sign Language,* ed. by Stokoe, Croneberg and Casterline, (Washington, D.C., Gallaudet College Press), 313-319.
The Deaf American,
Official (monthly) publication of the National Association of the Deaf.
Ervin-Tripp, Susan,
1964   "An Analysis of the Interaction of Language, Topic, and Listener", *American Anthropologist* 66, 86-102.
Fabray, Nanette,
1968   "Testimony of N. Fabray before House Subcommittee, July 16, 1968", *The Deaf American* 20, 16-20.
Ferguson, Charles A.,
1959   "Diglossia", *Word* 15, 325-340 (Reprinted in *Language in Culture and Society,* ed. by Hymes [New York, Harper and Row]).
Fitzgerald, Edith,
1929   *Straight Language for the Deaf* (Staunton, Va.) (11th printing 1965, Washington, D.C., The Volta Bureau).
Gorman, Pierre Paul,
1960   "Certain Social and Psychological Difficulties Facing the Deaf Person in the English Community", Unpublished Ph.D. Dissertation (Cambridge University).
Kakamasu, James,
1968   "Urubú Sign Language", *IJAL* 34, 275-281.
Ljung, M.,
1965   "Principles of a Stratificational Analysis of the Plains Indian Sign Language", *IJAL* 31, 119-127.
McNeill, David,
1966   "Developmental Psycholinguistics", *The Genesis of Language,* ed. by Smith and Miller (Cambridge, Mass., M.I.T. Press), 15-84.
Meadow, Kathryn,
1968   "Early Manual Communication in Relation to the Deaf Child's Intellectual, Social, and Communicative Functioning", *American Annals of the Deaf* 113, 29-41.
Northampton charts, in Yale, Caroline A.,
1925   *Formation and Development of English Elementary Sounds* (Northampton, Mass., Gazette Printing Co.).
Quigley, Stephen P.,
. n.d.   "The Influence of Fingerspelling on the Development of Language, Communication, and Educational Achievement in Deaf Children" (Urbana, Ill.) (Mimeo).
Sebeok, Thomas A.,
1969   "Semiotics and Ethology", *The Linguistic Reporter* suppl. 22, 9-15 (partially reprinted from *Approaches to Animal Communication,* ed. by Sebeok and

Ramsay [The Hague, Mouton, 1969].

Stokoe, William, C., Jr., C. Croneberg and D. Casterline,
1965   *A Dictionary of American Sign Language* (Washington, D.C., Gallaudet College Press).

Williams, Judith S.,
1968   *Bilingual Experiences of a Deaf Child* (= ED 030 092 6p. MF $ 0.25, HC $ 0.40 in *Research in Education,* 1970).

Wing, George W.,
1887   "The Theory and Practice of Grammatical Methods", *American Annals of the Deaf* 32, 84-89.

INDEX

Page numbers in italics refer to full bibliographical citation.

APPROACHES TO SEMIOTICS

edited by

THOMAS A. SEBEOK

Prices are subject to change
Titles without prices are in preparation

MOUTON · PUBLISHERS · THE HAGUE